The Life and Legacy of Mary McLeod Bethune
Nancy Ann Zrinyi Long

I dedicate this book to my husband, who for over thirty-two years has supported me in my pursuit of projects, activities, and adventures. This is also for my father, Ted Zrinyi, who has always been a role model for the values of hard work and perseverance.

For information address
The Florida Historical Society
435 Brevard Avenue
Cocoa, Florida 32922
www.florida-historical-soc.org

Manufactured in the United States of America
ISBN 1-886104-14-X

Published by
The Florida Historical Society Press
435 Brevard Avenue
Cocoa, FL 32935
phone (321) 690-0099
wynne@flahistory.net
www.floridabooks.net

FLORIDA HISTORICAL SOCIETY
P·R·E·S·S

TABLE OF CONTENTS

Forward

This book is easy and interesting reading. It presents the "Life and Legacy" of the late Dr. Mary McLeod Bethune holistically and concludes with testimonies from living witnesses. The author narrates Dr. Bethune's early years and documents how developments in those years influenced her later accomplishments. Permeating Dr. Bethune's spectacular career is a philosophy based on deep religious convictions and held that "work was honorable, no matter how menial the task."

This volume delineates and illuminates the dimensions of Dr. Bethune's life and work and focuses on her persistence in the face of numerous challenges. She is presented as an educator, politician, international figure, advisor to presidents of the United States, participant in the work of the Red Cross and United Nations. Her appointment to the position of Director of Negro Affairs in the National Youth Administration by President Roosevelt and her persistent toils for a society of justice are described in language that holds the reader's attention. In addition to Dr. Bethune's labors as college president and later Director of Negro Affairs, she was very active with women's issues. This led to the founding of the National Council of Negro Women – an organization that remains very active under the current leadership of Dr. Dorothy I. Height.

This book takes on new meaning and interest as the author arranges for persons who knew and experienced Dr. Bethune to share their impressions of the lady who meant so much to so many. This list includes family members, colleagues in the academic community, graduates of Bethune-Cookman College, and others who were greatly influenced by Dr. Bethune's dedication and hard work. For those who want to know Dr. Bethune and to understand her profound sense of mission, this book, *The Life and Legacy of Mary McLeod Bethune*, is must reading.

Dr. Oswald P. Bronson
President of Bethune-Cookman College
July 19, 2004

Acknowledgments and Sources

Having lived in Daytona Beach since 1972, I had heard little about Bethune-Cookman College, and I had never even seen the campus until I was hired to teach there in 1992. Walking around the campus, I began to find "treasures" popping up in the ground, and that is when I learned about the school being built on an old dump. I started to talk to older people who had known Dr. Bethune, look more closely at the old buildings, and then learned that my office had actually been an operating room in the first black hospital in the city. I became interested in the sorely-needed restoration effort that the College Women Association was conducting at the Foundation. I began to interview individuals who gave their first hand accounts of Dr. Bethune, as I realized that these elderly people were gold mines of historical information that had not been recorded.

These interviews provided material for my research, as well as the book *Mary McLeod Bethune: A Biography* by Rackham Holt, which was published in 1964. Ms. Holt did extensive interviews with Dr. Bethune before her death, and her book is actually the only biography about Dr. Bethune's personal life other than a few books written for children. The interviews, Ms. Holt's biography, and the Mary McLeod Bethune Papers stored in the Bethune-Cookman College Library Archives are the main sources for this biography. I also credit the book by Audrey Thomas McCluskey and Elaine Smith entitled *Mary McLeod Bethune: Building Better World* as providing insight into this phenomenal woman who was able to accomplish so much and affect so many people in her eighty years of life.

Prologue

July 10, 1875 — May 18, 1955

Mary McLeod Bethune slowly walked out to the balcony that overlooked the campus grounds. She rested on her favorite cane, the one that had once belonged to Franklin Delano Roosevelt and that had been given to Mary by Eleanor Roosevelt when her husband died. Mary was approaching eighty years old, and despite her asthma and heart problems, she still pushed herself to be active. The time spent in her beloved home, *Retreat*, was peaceful. Her grandchildren were often with her and she also made walks around the Bethune-Cookman College campus where she enjoyed the sight of the fruits of her labor. She had started this school with $1.50 and five little girls. Now it was a thriving accredited college with nearly 1000 students and many lovely buildings.

As she gazed out over the green campus and the large oaks, she recalled the dreams of her youth that had encouraged her. Throughout her life, she often talked about the three dreams that had motivated her.

The first dream came to her as a young girl suffering from an illness. She was standing on the bank of the St. Johns River wondering how to get across. Behind her, she saw a large army of young people coming toward her. Someone approached her and said, "You are planning to cross this river, but before you cross it you must take this book and register the names of all those young people that you see in the distance." Later a friend interpreted this dream for her. It meant that she was destined to undertake a great work for young people and that for many years, she would be spared to lead these young people on to great accomplishments.

The second dream also placed her at the edge of the St. Johns River. Mary's mother and father were on one side and Dr. Satterfield, president of Scotia Seminary, on the other side. They locked arms with her and the group began to wade out into the current. Her parents went so far and then her mother turned to her and said, "My child, we have brought you as far as we can go, but now we must leave you and you must make it yourself." Then Dr. Satterfield went on deeper into the water with her until he said, "Mary, I have brought you to the distance I can go; now you will have to make the balance of the way yourself." She interpreted this to mean these people had prepared her for a life of service and she was to go on into the river or world to fulfill this mission.

In the final dream, she found herself on the bank of the Halifax River in Daytona, praying for a way to build her school. A man came galloping down the street on a beautiful horse. He was dressed in a uniform and jumped off the horse, asking her, "What are you sitting here for?" She replied, "I am just trying to see my way clear to build my school." He said, "I am Booker T. Washington." He reached in his hip pocket and pulled out a parcel in a soiled handkerchief, evidently used for mopping off the perspiration, and out of this handkerchief he unwrapped a large diamond. He said, "Take this and build your school." He mounted the horse and rode off. Mary thought, "This was my first contact with Booker T. Washington except for my reading of all that he was doing in building Tuskegee. I felt that this diamond represented confidence, will power, stick-to-it-iveness, work, suffering, friends, doubt, wisdom, common sense—everything necessary for the building of a beautiful Bethune-Cookman."

These dreams inspired her and as she stood there in the twilight years of her life, breathing in the fresh morning air tinged with the scent of orange blossoms, Mary realized the dreams had come true. What an exciting life she had led! Starting as a small child picking cotton in the fields near her home in Mayesville, South Carolina, she felt great satisfaction in her many accomplishments. Her life had been blessed with rich experiences and incredible achievements. Her motto had been "Not for oneself, but for others." She had accomplished her dreams!

Chapter 1

The Early Years

*"Our greatest objective is to live for God
and bring others to do so."*

On May 18, 1955, when Mary McLeod Bethune died, she was considered one of the greatest black women to have lived. The *Christian Century* said that "the story of her life should be taught to every school child." The *Pittsburgh Courier* stated "In any race or nation she would have been an outstanding personality and made a noteworthy contribution because her chief attribute was her indomitable soul." The *Washington Post* commented that "Not only her own people but all America has been enriched and ennobled by her courageous, ebullient spirit."

How could a poor black woman, 15th of 17 children, raised by former slaves, achieve such prestige? Furthermore, she achieved this fame at a time when very dark-skinned persons with heavy Afro-American features were looked down upon. Despite the extreme poverty and prejudice she faced, Mary McLeod Bethune became one of the greatest Americans of her time. What was her secret?—her deep faith in God and herself. These are her words, "Faith is the first factor in a life devoted to service. Without faith, nothing is possible, Faith in God is the greatest Power...but great, too, is faith in oneself."

Her parents, Patsy and Samuel McLeod, were slaves on the same plantation; they had fourteen children who were spread out on various plantations. After the Civil War ended and all were freed, the family gradually gathered the children together and managed to buy five acres near Mayesville, South Carolina. Patsy McLeod had continued to work for the family who had owned her as a slave and she saved enough money to buy the land from her former owner.

Patsy McLeod was a strong woman who was an excellent organizer with great creativity. A small woman with delicate features, she was uneducated but always spoke with perfect diction and carried herself with great dignity. Samuel McLeod was a sturdy medium-sized individual who believed in hard work and caring for his family. Unlike many black families during slavery, the McLeods were a devoted couple and all the children had the same father,

Samuel and Patsy McLeod, Mary's Parents

which was a big issue for Patsy, a devout Christian who raised the children to be proud of family and race. She was supposedly the descendant of a ruling family in Africa and she instilled a pride of ancestry into her children.

Father and sons built a four-room log cabin, and this is where Mary was born. Two siblings were born after her. Mary's parents felt that she was just different from rest of her brothers and sisters. The midwife declared that the child had been born with her eyes wide-open; her parents felt that this child born in freedom was destined to follow a special path. She was iron-willed and dark skinned like her mother, but she got her robustness from her father. At an early age, she showed independence and strong drive. She was a leader of even the older children. She was not what some would consider an attractive child with her dark broad features, but even at a young age her charismatic personality and positive attitude attracted people. She also showed great compassion for others and she always wanted to share with others, whether it was soup for a sick person or giving her own shoes away to someone who had none. She was intelligent and showed a great desire to learn. The McLeod family prospered due to their hard efforts. All children had assigned chores and worked in the fields raising food crops, cotton, and rice. The homestead was well kept and the McLeods raised the children to value cleanliness and neatness. Patsy was a leader in the area, often serving as midwife or nurse to neighbors. They were generous to those in need, and they

Small cabin where Dr. Bethune was born and raised as the fifteenth of seventeen children born to former slaves in Mayesville, South Carolina.

were leaders in the Mayesville Church, which they traveled five miles to attend every Sunday. The children were raised with discipline and love and strong Christian values, especially the girls who were taught the importance of chastity and self-respect.

Patsy had a large burn scar on her chest caused by her master's son who threw a ladle of hot candle wax at her when she resisted his advances. She told this story to impress upon her girls pride in themselves; she did not want them to be taken advantage of by the sweet-talking young men. Every one of the McLeod daughters married young but properly with a church wedding in the family's yard.

The McLeod home was a gathering place for neighbors and Samuel McLeod was known for his great singing voice and love of music that he instilled in his children. Mary developed into a strong soprano who was very at ease singing in front of people. Traveling preachers would often stop in and the neighbors would gather for sermons. This is how Mary first heard about missionaries going to Africa to work with the natives and this became her dream. The McLeod home was also the site for many "moonlight" parties, which were social gatherings after a hard day of corn husking, cotton harvesting, or sugar cane gathering. White and black sharecroppers and farmers shared these festivities as color lines blurred with the need to get work done. Likewise blacks and whites would go to work at the former masters' plantations when help was needed to harvest crops, and usually all would attend the hog-killing party where there would be food, music, and dancing. The community that Mary grew up in was a friendly mix where the races blended, but the distinctions would rise at times. Her first real encounter with racism occurred one July day when she accompanied her father as he drove a wagon of produce to the Mayesville market. The market was filled with a friendly crowd of people, with men drinking and joking as they bargained. But then a drunken loud-mouthed black man named Gus had an encounter with a drunken white man who ordered him to blow out a match that he held close to Gus' face. When Gus pushed the man's hands away, the man fell to the ground. Suddenly the atmosphere changed and someone yelled for a rope as a few white men grabbed Gus' arms. Samuel McLeod immediately hurried Mary to the wagon and ordered her not to turn around as he quickly drove out of town. This was Mary's first encounter with the practice of lynching.

One day Mary accompanied her mother to the former master's home as her mother continued to work for the Wilsons after her emancipation. Mary went to the playhouse in the yard with the Wilson children. She picked up a book, and one of the girls told her to go get a picture book because Mary could not read. This instilled in her a burning desire to do what they could—read a book. Mary became determined to become educated.

Mary was brought up with deep religious convictions, being taught that God did not discriminate and all things were possible through him. Her religion helped her cope with a hard life as a youth. From a very early age, she worked at picking cotton 10-12 hours a day. All the family and black neighbors were illiterate because there were no black schools or education for the ex-slaves in the area. She desperately wanted to attend schools like the white children and learn to read. Then one day a mission teacher Emma Jane Wilson came to the farm to announce that she was starting a school five miles away in Mayesville. At the age of seven, Mary convinced her father to let her go to school despite the fact he needed hands in the cotton field. The family decided that they could spare one child from the fieldwork and they let Mary attend the school. She would walk the five miles to and from school, thrilled finally to be able to learn to read and write. Education was very important to her, and she proved herself to be a hard-working intelligent student. This first school was a small church with homemade benches and tables. Miss Wilson was kind and patient with the students as they learned the basic 3Rs. On Sundays, Mary would share what she had learned with the other children. She taught her older brother to read and she delighted her parents who, for the first time, had someone in the household who could read them newspapers and the Bible. Her skill in math led to her helping her father and others, even white farmers, as she calculated the fair price for their cotton.

Walking the five miles to and from school was no hardship for Mary with her eagerness to learn. There was another incident that did make her aware of racism. Some of the white boys had begun to harass the few young black children who walked to school. Mary began to place rocks on top of the books in her school bag. One day this group of white boys began to call her names and then they unleashed their large dog to attack her. She grabbed a stick and swung at the dog as she began to run. The dog tore off Mary's skirt as she grabbed rocks from her bag and threw them over her head at the boys. They yelled "Naked *nigger!*" at her and then called the dog back and retreated. The crying Mary ran home. Later Mr. Cooper, the boys' father, met Mary's mother at the road and he promised the boys would not bother Mary again. He also added that blacks would never learn anything except in the cotton fields. This only encouraged Mary to work harder in school.

After 6th grade, she wanted to attend Scotia Seminary, but the family mule died and they needed to buy another. There was no money for her tuition, but the family prayed. Mary returned to working in the cotton fields for a year. Then in October 1891, her teacher, a Miss Wilson, came to the "Homestead" to announce that a white Quaker woman from Denver, Colorado, named Mary Chrisman was interested in the black children in South Carolina since she had seen some literature about the education effort. This teacher and dressmaker decided to give a scholarship for a young girl's education, and Mary had been chosen for this scholarship. Years later, Mary wrote, "To this day, my heart thrills with gratitude at the memory of that day when a poor dressmaker, sewing for her daily bread, heard my call and came to my assistance. Out of her scanty earnings, she invested in a life — my life!" Mary tore off her cotton sack, fell on her knees, and thanked God for this opportunity. Her father got her an old trunk and neighbors helped with knitting socks and sewing some items for her. The day she took the train from Mayesville, several neighbors joined the family to wish her good luck and see her off.

She arrived at Scotia Seminary in Concord, North Carolina, and was taken to a beautiful brick building where she had a lovely room shared with her roommate, Janie Shankle, and later Abbie Greeley. The next morning she went with Janie to a dining room with tablecloths and silverware. This was a new world for Mary, but she soon learned etiquette and adapted to this school environment. She became popular with the teachers and students, worked hard on any chores given, and joined the chorus and debating team. This was her first close contact with white people, and the white teachers were especially supportive of Mary. One teacher, a Miss Cathcart, who taught mathematics and music, helped supply her with clothing and shoes. There was only one time that she was disciplined — she was running down the stairs and ran right into the principal, Dr. David Satterfield. He told her running in the halls was prohibited and she received three demerits. Fifteen demerits and a girl would be sent home! She followed him to his office to apologize and received a short lecture that she must always be a good example of behavior for her race. Mary was so tearfully contrite that the principal rescinded the demerits and she was never in trouble again at the school.

Mary attended Scotia for seven years. All students had chores and one of Mary's jobs was to ring the bell. She was so punctual about the warning bells for wake-up, class, meals, and bedtime that her title was the "Bell Ringer of Scotia." She became so well-known for her dependability and responsible attitude that she was assigned the special honor of ironing Dr. Satterfield's shirts. During the summers, Mary worked for white families at their summer homes. She not only earned money, which she sent home to the family, but she learned skills in homemaking and childcare.

Mary was outgoing and well liked at the school. She was president of the literary society and a member of the debate team. Although her grades were average in her subjects and she struggled in math, Mary excelled in music as she worked to develop her clear soprano voice. When Mary graduated in 1894, her benefactor Miss Chrisman sent a Bible and a photograph of herself. Miss Chrisman then offered to continue her financial support when Mary received a scholarship to the Dwight Moody Institute for Home and Foreign Missions in Chicago.

Of the thousand students at Moody, Mary was the only black. She truly felt she was destined to become a missionary to Africa. A part of her training included the assignment to go out among the people in Chicago, sometime in areas of derelicts and drug users, and proselytize. She would deliver speeches at the Mission Room, which was located in the poor section, and also sing hymns at the police station at noon. One evening she was invited into a home where a dozen men and women were drinking and playing cards. They began to make fun of her and actually locked the door to bar her leaving. After joking and teasing the frightened new missionary, the woman who had invited her in told the group to let Mary leave. Mary returned after dark to the institute where teachers and friends had been worried and praying for her. Ironically a week later she met the same woman who told her that the men had only been teasing her; the woman and some of her friends wanted to attend the church and Mary warmly invited and welcomed them.

She now was the soloist at the Sunday services. She also traveled to the Midwest in the spring as a "gospel train" took the young people to areas where there was a need for Sunday schools. Mary was the first black woman that many of these westerners had ever seen. Returning from this trip, Mary, at the age of nineteen, completed her training at the Bible Institute, and she applied to the Mission Board of the Presbyterian Church. She was told that there were no openings for Negroes in Africa. At first, she was greatly disappointed and although her music teacher told her she could be a great success as a concert singer, Mary wanted to be an educator. She returned home to Mayesville and worked at the mission school where she had begun her education. Her work as a teacher made her realize that African-Americans needed God and school as much as Negroes in Africa.

Chapter 2

The Educator

"Let there be light, two kinds of light: to light the outside world, to light the world within the soul. Each generation with its own lamp gave out the lamp of learning, education."

Mary returned to Mayesville, South Carolina, where she assisted Miss Wilson, her former teacher, at the mission school. She then moved to Atlanta, Georgia, where she began teaching at the Haines Normal and Industrial School under the supervision of her former teacher, Lucy Croft Laney. Mary sent her entire teaching salary home to cover tuition for her two younger sisters to go to school and to help her parents pay off their debts. The Presbyterian Board then sent her to Sumter, South Carolina, to the Kindell Institute where she taught and worked in social services. She was active in the church and here she met her future husband, Albertus Bethune, at a church choir practice. He had a beautiful tenor voice and was involved with the church activities. He had been born in South Carolina, had a fine family upbringing, and was interested in business. He had been a student at Avery Institute in Charleston, South Carolina, but he quit school just before his senior year to help provide money for his younger brother to enter school. He taught school but later became a haberdasher. After a year of dating, Mary took Albertus to Mayesville to meet her parents and also see the new weatherboard house that her father had built to replace the log cabin. The family approved of Albertus and they married in 1898. Their only son Albert was born one year later on February 3, 1899—Patsy and Samuel's ninetieth grandchild.

Mary had a quiet year from active work. She was engaged in civic activities while caring for her baby. Then she became acquainted with a Reverend C. Uggans from Palatka, Florida. He talked to her about the need to start a school there as so little was being done for Blacks in that region. She headed to Palatka when Albert was nine months old. Her husband joined her and they rented a small house on Lemon Street near the church. For five years she worked to build a community school, visited the jails, went to talk with the sawmill workers at their homes and jobs, and visited the clubs where the youths hung out. She sold insurance policies for the Afro-American Life

7

Insurance Company to earn extra income.

She still wanted to open her own school. She talked with a Reverend Pratt who had traveled around Florida, and he suggested Daytona Beach, which was fifty miles southeast of Palatka. When Henry Flagler's Florida East Coast Railway began construction, black laborers gathered in Daytona Beach. Mary realized the children of these workers would need an education. Rev. Pratt also told her that Daytona was a growing tourist town whose winter residents might provide a source of financial support for her school. She took the train to Daytona and met with a friend of Rev. Pratt, Mrs. Susie Warren. Mrs. Warren had three daughters and was very supportive of Mary's goal of opening a school for girls in

Thomas White of the White Sewing Machine Company became a generous supporter of the school; White Hall, the main administrative building on campus today, is named in his memory.

the area. At that time, the only education offered to blacks was a kindergarten begun by a group of white women called the Palmetto Club. These women wintered in Daytona, and had started the kindergarten primarily as a place for black youngsters to stay while their mothers worked at the women's homes. Mrs. Warren took Mary on a tour of the poor black section of Daytona where she found dense ignorance, meager educational facilities, deep racial prejudice, crime and violence. She then met John Williams, one of the few black landowners in the area. He owned a two-story frame house near the railroad and he agreed to rent it to Mary for eleven dollars a month. She only had a dollar and a half for a down payment, but Mr. Williams said he trusted her, agreed to the rental and assured her the men who were living in the house, workers on the construction of the Clarendon Hotel, would leave at the end of the month and find other rooms. She planned to return to Palatka and pack up their belongings when a letter arrived from Albertus. During her absence, a fire destroyed the family's dwelling and possessions in Palatka, which Mary saw as a definite sign that God wanted her to go to Daytona. Henry Flagler continued building his railroad and many more blacks were migrating to Daytona for work. Mary came to the East Side of Florida in 1904 and began to address the problem that there was no education available for the black boys and girls in Daytona. Mary planned to capitalize on the fact that Daytona was the summer home for wealthy people like James Gamble of the Proctor and Gamble Company, Thomas White of the White Sewing Machine Company in Cleveland, and the wealthy white women who had formed the philanthropic Palmetto Club. She realized these people could be used as a support group for her dreams.

Her son was five at the time when the family found a place to live with Mrs. Warren, who was a strong supporter of this effort to start a school in the Daytona area. Mary went around the neighborhood begging for boxes to make benches and stools and other items to start the school. The three Warren daughters were the first little girls enrolled in the school. On October 4, 1904, the school started in the rented building owned by John Williams. She had five students — Lucille, Lena, Ruth, Anna, and Celeste, as well as her own son, Albert. No one thought the school would last long. However Mary, who was now twenty-nine years of age, began to get increased enrollment of children of working mothers who wanted their children safe during the day while the mothers worked as maids, cooks, and laundresses. Tuition was fifty cents a week. Mr. Williams gave her an old double bed frame which she painted, stuffed with moss, and turned into a sleeping place for children whose mothers had to travel with the white families on trips, leaving the children in Mary's safekeeping. More people in the neighborhood began to help out with donations of items or skills, and families, who could not always pay the tuition, donated food and work in lieu of money. Mary was able to pay the monthly rent. She also began to offer night classes in reading and writing to adults to improve the literacy rate for local blacks. These adults paid if they could or traded work at the school for lessons.

Thus, the Daytona Literary and Industrial School for Training Negro Girls was established. Some have questioned the legend of the school's founding. Dr. Marion Speight, who started teaching at Bethune-Cookman College in 1936, recalls that the story as told by Dr. Bethune would sometimes change, and it depended on the audience as to how much she would embellish the story. She was a dynamic speaker and storyteller who could emotionally capture an audience. Mary, with her charismatic appeal and persuasive manner, had been able to get support from not only the blacks in the area, but also from concerned whites that gave money for charitable causes. Thus, Dr. Bethune was able to start this school with only her personality, her energy, her effort, and very little money.

The philosophy which guided Mary's life was that work was honorable, no

9

matter how menial the task. She had always done any chore, whether it was cotton picking on the farm or floor scrubbing at the school, with effort and pride. At a time when blacks were trying to overcome the effects of slavery and become educated and skilled, Mary felt that the youth needed to begin their education by learning a trade. Like Booker T. Washington who had founded Tuskegee Institute, she felt young girls should learn agriculture, industry, and domestic skills to better themselves. She was trying to teach them practical knowledge of etiquette and hygiene, as well as a trade that would allow them to get work and earn a living. She was criticized by some for not pushing students into higher academic and scientific studies at the school. One incident occurred when she attended church and the preacher saw her in the pew and focused on her endeavors at the school. He preached that she was teaching girls' hands but not their minds. He continued that he would rather see his daughter taught by the devil than by Mary. This attitude represented the chasm in approaches to black education. Mary and Booker T. Washington believed that the majority of blacks were so impoverished and undereducated that they first needed to learn the basic skills of how to function in society and earn a living before they should earn a higher education. She was in no way saying blacks could not achieve higher levels of intellectual development, but being practical, she worked to help the average poor youth learn to become self-sufficient and socially adept.

This first school started with packing crates found at the dump or donated, burnt sticks used as charcoal for pencils, ink made from mashed elderberries, and meat wrapping paper from a butcher's shop. Mary had faith, but she also believed God helped those who helped themselves. She had many incidents occur in which faith in God seemed to be the only answer to difficult problems. She had no dishes at first and a friend loaned her enough for the little girls and her son at Christmas. Then the friend reneged and needed the dishes returned. As Mary packed the dishes for return, there was a knock at the door and there a Mrs. Thompson stood with a set of dishes she no longer needed since her son had given her a new set for Christmas. Another incident that reinforced Mary's faith happened on a Saturday when she had no food. She went to a nearby store, but was not allowed to get any more food on credit. When she returned to the schoolhouse, four men were sitting on the porch. They had been attending the night classes she offered in reading. They paid her eight dollars in appreciation of her efforts to educate them, and she immediately went to the store with money for food for the children.

Besides the school and the night classes, training was provided to the larger African-American community on basic cleanliness, housework, counseling, and other ways to improve the standard of living. Blacks were encouraged to keep their yards clean and houses neat, as signs of pride in themselves. Mary was against drinking alcohol as she had seen its destructive effects on people and families, so she began to hold Loyal Temperance League meetings on Sunday afternoons. She would give a talk, bring in role models and discuss the contributions and pride of the Negroes, and sing folk songs and spirituals. One Sunday, a woman who had come to Daytona to work attended the meeting. After listening to the singers, she offered Mary an old foot-pedal harmonium if she could find a way to bring it from the woman's home in Jacksonville. People in the group helped, and the organ was shipped down and became a fixture in the Sunday temperance meetings.

One morning Mary was in the store when she began to talk with a white woman named Mrs. Maley. This woman bought the groceries for the children that day and encouraged Mary to meet with the Palmetto Club women and discuss her school project. These women agreed to help and set up the first advisory board with Mrs. Maley being the first president. Although the Negro neighborhood tried to assist the school, Mary decided to reach out to the wealthier white people in order to get the funds she needed. She began to simply knock on doors and tell people about the school and ask for support. There were times when she was rebuffed and humiliated, but she needed funds. She enrolled her son in the kindergarten run by the Palmetto Club, and she befriended Mrs. Mary Eliza Thompson who was the club president. Later Mr. Thompson became a staunch supporter of the school and joined the Board of Trustees.

The reputation of the school spread and more students wanted to attend. Mr. Williams owned a barn near the schoolhouse, and he agreed to rent it to Mary for expansion of the school. She had the girls gather useful junk from the surrounding area and worked to furnish and upgrade the barn for classrooms and sleeping quarters. She talked to Reverend Cromatia, who was a real estate agent, and they drove around the town to find a property where Mary could set up a permanent school with room for expansion. On the edge of the Negro neighborhood was an old dump referred to as "Hell's Hole." The cost of the land was $250. Mary had a fund raising ice cream social, and went to talk with the owner, a German named Mr. Kinsey. She had about $5 in change, which she dumped on the table from her handkerchief, and asked if that would be enough for down payment. Mr. Kinsey decided she was honest and agreed to the deal verbally. The only paperwork signed was when he turned over the deed to her when she made her last payment.

Work began immediately to clear the junk piles and level the land for building. As the students and hired men cleaned up the dumpsite, she continued to solicit support from the wealthier whites. Often the adults she tutored were gardeners and workers for the estates across the Halifax River on beachside. They would tell their employers about the school and arrange for Mary to meet with the employers so that she could ask for support. She acquired a second hand bicycle which she rode around the town and expanded her outreach for the school. The school now enrolled twenty girls.

One of the black workers told her he worked for James Gamble, owner of the Procter and Gamble Company in Cincinnati, Ohio. She wrote Mr. Gamble a note asking for a meeting and he agreed to have her come to his home. Instead of asking for funds, she asked him to become a trustee in her dream for a school. Mary arranged a meeting with Gamble, the mayor of Daytona, E. L. Smith, a realtor Laurence Thompson, and two Negro ministers Reverend James and Reverend Cromatia. The group met at the school where they sat on the two chairs and box crates. Students sang a few songs and recited verses for the men, and then Mary explained her dream for a permanent school. She then showed them the site she had chosen, and asked that they join her board of trustees for the school. Mr. Gamble agreed to be the chairman, Mr. Thompson the treasurer, and Reverend

James Gamble of the Proctor and Gamble empire was very impressed with Dr. Behtune. She appeared on his doorstep one day and asked him to be a "trustee of a dream," and soon he was president of the school's Board of Trustees.

James the secretary. A charter was drawn up and Mr. Gamble had his own attorney, Bert Fish, contribute his legal services. Legend goes that when Mr. Gamble asked where this school was, she replied, "In my mind and in my soul!" Gamble became one of her leading supporters and advocates. He became a friend who took an interest in her well-being.

Mr. Gamble attended church with Mr. George Doane, a retired businessman. They arranged for her to give a talk at the Stewart Methodist Church. After listening to her talk and observing the well-behaved students who accompanied her that day, Doane became a financial supporter and an advocate for the school in the community. Mary then approached Mrs. Howard, the owner of the Howard Hotel, with her plan to present music programs on beachside for the wealthy winter visitors. She took her students over and they sang songs and she herself performed medleys, along with her quartet, which consisted of herself, her husband, and two friends. The students would distribute flyers about the school, and then a basket would be passed for collections. The group performed next at the Hamilton Hotel, owned by Mrs. I. Maybette, whose daughter was so impressed with the students and the dream that she joined the Board of Trustees. These performances became exceedingly popular and raised much-needed funds for the school.

At one performance at the Palmetto Hotel, Mary attracted another supporter named Thomas White, president of the White Sewing Machine Company. After hearing her speech, he placed a $20 bill into the collection basket. Then one Saturday, as she was riding her bicycle on her way to solicit funds in the area, a white automobile pulled up alongside her. The chauffeur stopped the car and the distinguished looking, white-haired gentleman inside asked her if he could see her school. She quickly pedaled back to Faith Hall, a dormitory that was under construction and unfinished, but into which the female students had moved in September 1907. He found the place neat and clean but with walls that needed plastering and woodwork undone. Mary explained that funds were scarce and that work could only be done when the workmen could be paid. The school's larders were low on the grits, beans, and rice that were the main staples for meals; cornmeal was the only food she had to feed the girls that day. Mr. White also learned that the students were sleeping on straw matting from the dump. He remarked on the rickety old Singer sewing machine that stood in the hall, but was assured that it was the only machine the school had and that it was put to good use. When the tour was complete, Mary asked him to sign the school's guest book. He wrote, "This is the most heart warming thing I have seen in Florida." He then wrote out a check for two hundred dollars for supplies and also paid for a mason and a carpenter to complete the building. He ordered a new top-of-the-line White sewing machine for the school to replace the old machine he had seen.

White was a busy businessman, but often visited the school and took a personal interest in the happenings there. One cold day he learned the students were sleeping under their own coats for warmth, so he personally went to a store and purchased a large supply of blankets and linens for the students. He became a generous supporter and gave one thousand dollars to provide for the drainage of the swamp water that seeped into the well used for drinking water. With Gamble, he later contributed a cottage for the McLeod Hospital, beds for students, and funding for the Bethune home and Faith Hall. He died in 1914 but left a trust fund for the school, which led to the first brick structure on campus, White Hall, built and dedicated in 1918.

Despite the support of the winter tourists and the community, raising money for the school was a constant problem. Mary continued to ride her second-hand bicycle all over Daytona, telling people about the school and asking for help. Students made pies and ice cream to sell. Students continued to sing at hotels and churches on beachside where the wealthy vacationed, and then Mary would speak to the individuals about her school and ask for support. Enrollment at the school, which she called the Daytona Literary and Industrial School for Training Negro Girls, grew rapidly to nearly one hundred students.

Hell's Hole was slowly being transformed into a campus with flowers and trees replacing junk and underbrush. One section was turned into a farm, which the girls ran. They raised vegetables for canning and selling. Meat from cows, hogs, and chickens was stored for student use. Students ground syrup cane. Mary's brother came to the school to help the girls learn farming techniques. Mary believed in educating heart, head, and mind and each girl learned a means of livelihood. This first building Faith Hall was a four-story frame house that served every need—dormitory, classrooms, dining room, and laundry. A small building, which served as the kitchen and science building, was acquired next, and then a small cottage used for production of bas-

This brick building replaced the original wooden Faith Hall which was the first school house built on campus in 1907.

kets, rugs, brooms, and music instruction.

Even with support from the community and benefactors, Mary was constantly facing obstacles of low funds and growing student needs. Money for food and supplies continued to be an ever-present problem. Yet her faith never wavered and she always felt the Lord would provide. One morning, she believed her faith in God reaped special benefits when she and the children prayed hard for food because there was none in the larder. Before the service was over, a wagon pulled up in front of the building with vegetables that a friend had sent over. For her, this was proof that God was watching over her efforts. When Mary needed a roof repair, but had no money, she prayed and then instructed some helpers to build a scaffold with the last of the materials. As the men were building the scaffold, a letter came from a friend who sent a check for a thousand dollars. Mary gathered the workers around for a prayer of thanks. Then the money was used to purchase what was needed to repair the roof. These incidents and others like them reinforced Mary's deep faith in God and convinced her of the fact that she was following the path that she was destined to follow.

Mary found another supporter in Margaret Rhodes, who had a winter home in Daytona. She joined the Women's Advisory Board and later became a member of the Board of Trustees. Her brother was Harrison Garfield Rhodes, a playwright and author. He came up with the idea of a Christmas activity as a fundraiser. The girls dressed in white with white scarves over their heads and they carried lanterns around the neighborhoods as they sang Christmas carols. This practice quickly became a custom for the Daytona area and residents would put candles in the window to show the group led by Dr. Bethune that they were welcome to sing at the house.

She also took on demands of community service by establishing a mission at a migrant workers' camp on the outskirts of the city, where she took students to sing, teach, and help the poor living there. These camps were hastily built shacks put up about five miles from town for the men who cut down pine trees for turpentine. The conditions were filthy and whole families were often crammed into one-room shacks. Mary went to talk with the white owner of several camps, a Mr. Clark, who agreed to let her visit once a week. So, in 1907, Mary began the Tomoka Mission. Students and others in the community instructed children of the camps in scripture and gave classes in reading, singing, and sewing. The program grew as classes for mothers were offered with instruction on childcare, cleanliness, and health. Programs were given on Saturday afternoons to try to reach the men. These men were tough illiterates who resisted prayer services. Paydays were days Mary kept the girls away from the camps as drinking, fighting, and womanizing was the usual custom. But some reforms were made as the camp children walked back to the school with the students at times and were exposed to a better way of life. Arrangements were also made for some men and their families to attend the Community Service meetings on Sunday afternoons. Mr. Clark began to get involved by donating pencils and tablets to the school at Christmas and he supported the Christmas party given for the camp workers by giving gifts of clothing to the adults. The Tomoka Mission actually lasted for five years and moved three times, always farther west, as the laborers were forced to move to camps closer to the tree supply. Finally, Mary went to the Volusia County School superintendent who went to the camps and saw the need for some kind of education for the children. The county set up a small school near the camps, so the children had some type of education, even if it was only for three months of the year.

She started the Better Boys Club to help the young black boys in the city learn to become better citizens. She persuaded Mr. Doane to build a small cottage on a rented vacant lot and this became a center for social activities for boys. The club had projects such as neighborhood and yard cleanup with prizes for the cleanest areas. One young boy who was positively influenced by the club was Howard Thurman, who later became a well-known professor and preacher at Boston University.

In 1909, Mary was in New York for several days of speeches. She was staying at an old boarding house when Mrs. Rose Keyser visited her. A widow who was the head of the White Rose Mission, a home for delinquent Negro girls, Mrs. Keyser was well educated, having graduated with honors from Hunter College. She had been a supervisor at a small school for troubled girls in Tallahassee before returning to New York to supervise the mission. The two women were in accord that education should include spiritual values as well as academics. Mrs. Keyser

Portrait of Dr. Bethune in her younger days.

agreed to move to Daytona where she took over the educational program, understanding that the pay would be very low. She was one of only a few qualified teachers in Florida at that time since most teachers had only an eighth-grade education. She efficiently ran the academic area of the school, acquiring better-trained teachers and helping raise the standards of the Daytona Institute, which now offered classes through the eighth grade. This freed Mary Bethune to pursue the role of fundraising and administration, for funding now consumed most of her time.

It was through Mrs. Keyser that Mary began her involvement with the National Association of Colored Women. She convinced Mary to attend the national conference to be held in Virginia at the Hampton Institute. At the meeting, influential black women from all over the country reported on events and projects in their states. Mary requested a few minutes to speak to the group. She gave an inspiring description of her efforts with the school and need for support; the group responded with a collection for the school. At this conference, Mary met Madame C. J. Walker, who was presenting her inventions of the pressing iron and oils that would make her the first successful black business woman in America and who opened up the career of beautician for black women. As her wealth grew, Madame Walker became a sponsor of the school and conducted successful fundraising drives for the education of blacks.

Later Mary wrote the Hampton Institute asking for their recommendation of a person who could teach handicrafts to students. Hampton recommended Miss Portia Smiley, who came to the school in 1909 and proved to be a goldmine of skills. She not only taught sewing, domestic skills, basketry, broom making, rug weaving, and beadwork, but she was also a practical nurse. Miss Smiley instigated the annual advisory board bazaar where students displayed and sold crafts, a tradition that continues today.

With the school safely in the hands of Mrs. Keyser and Miss Smiley, Mary could now travel farther and more often to raise funds. Her reputation grew, and, in 1910, she was awarded the first of her eleven honorary degrees, an honorary Master of Science from South Carolina State College.

When the Institute was seven years old, Mary proposed to the Board of Trustees that the school should expand to include a high school because some students who had completed the eighth grade wanted to continue with accredited high school courses. The meeting became emotionally heated as the trustees told Mary that eight years of schooling was enough for Negro children. Only Harrison Rhodes stood by her. Mary grew angry and asked one of the opposing Trustees if eight years of schooling was enough for his children. He hesitatingly replied that he expected more from them. "Why, then, will you not support the same education for black children?" she asked. The debate continued over limiting the expansion of the school. Mary, after pleading that black children deserved higher educational opportunities and also pointing out that the board was there to help her educate the youth and not hinder her efforts, simply walked out of the meeting with the declaration

Dr. Bethune's many awards displayed in the study.

she would just go and build another school if they were going to limit her.

Later that evening Mr. Gamble went to visit Mary. He told her he would support her efforts to start the high school. With his support, the others cooperated and the high school curriculum was established. Summer classes were also started for the young women teaching at the state schools, since few of the teachers at the Negro schools had more than an eighth grade certificate.

Five girls composed the first high school graduating class in 1915. One of the girls, Arabella Denniston, was skilled in business and became Bethune's personal secretary. She later worked for Mary in Washington and became the executive secretary for the National Council of Negro Women in 1935. Another graduate, Sadie Franklin, became a dietician and the executive housekeeper at Freedmen's Hospital in Washington. Mary was beginning the long legacy of successful educated blacks that contributed to society with their head, heart, and hands.

Another undertaking was the establishment of the first hospital for blacks in Daytona, which started as a two-bed room near the school. When a young student, Anita Pinkney, suffered an attack of appendicitis, the white hospital refused to help the child. The nearest hospital for blacks was in St. Augustine, fifty miles away. Mary implored Dr. C. C. Bohannon, the white doctor from the local hospital, to operate. Since the black child would not be admitted to an operating room, the doctor arranged for her to go to a screened-in porch in the rear of the hospital where he operated with Mary assisting. The next morning Mary went to visit the child and was told she would not be allowed to even enter the porch area. Dr. Bohannon, who was making his rounds, personally escorted Mary to the porch to see the child. Mary was so angry over this incident that it inspired her to push for the establishment of the first hospital for blacks. She went to Mr. White and convinced him to purchase two lots near Faith Hall. A new young doctor, T. A. Adams, had returned to Daytona after graduation and he helped open a two-bed hospital in the cottage that was on the lots. Later with support from Mr. White and Mr. Gamble, a twenty-six-bed hospital was constructed. This became the McLeod Hospital and the Training School for Nurses was later established in 1912. Twenty years later, this building was converted to into the Keyser Teaching Laboratory when the city allowed blacks admission to a segregated section of the new Halifax Hospital. Today it is known as the General Studies Building and serves as offices and classrooms for the Reading and Mathematics Departments.

Mary's supporters in Daytona were mainly winter visitors who encouraged her to visit the North where people could hear about the school and perhaps provide further sources of funding. Her first trip north was at the invitation of the Mellours in Pittsburgh, where she gave her first speech to an all-white audience. She told an anecdote which became a common thread in her speeches. It was the story of a northern missionary who was in the South and would be returning to the Mission Board with a report of what he observed. He asked the group of children what he should tell the people in the North. One young boy raised his hand and said, "Tell them we are rising!" Mary used this expression to describe the school in Daytona. The Mellours arranged speeches and home visits for her, and she realized the North was a great source of support for her school. Next, she went to Springfield, Illinois, and on the way, she met the train conductor, Stephen Chapin, who was a deacon at the Springfield First Congregational Church. He invited her to stay with his family and attend the prayer service that night. Mary gave an emotional speech and the black church members, though not wealthy, were generous in their support. They also decided to adopt the school as their missionary project.

Mary needed their help later when the owner of land next to the school approached her about buying the lot and cottage. He wanted an outrageous amount of $2500 for the land and threatened that if she did not buy, he had buyers who were not the kind of people Mary would want around the girls. Mary contacted the Chapins and the Springfield Church. They agreed to use the church savings to purchase the land for the school. The trustees of the school were called into a meeting and Mary explained the rational of the purchase of land as a step toward protecting the school. Some trustees felt the money could be better used, but she argued that the Board of Trustees did not understand the dangers and threats of the uneducated and unlawful individuals in the black community. She wanted the school and the girls protected; plus the money was earmarked for the land and should therefore be used as the Springfield people wanted. She won her argument. The land was bought and the cottage became known as Chapin Cottage. This building served as a faculty overflow area, and through the years it was moved as needed to serve as an isolation ward during a flu epidemic, a classroom setting for the Home Economics Department, and eventually the home for the college chaplain.

Booker T. Washington visited the school in 1912. Mary had always agreed with his views that blacks needed to learn a trade or skill in order to become successful in society. Washington encouraged her in her efforts to recruit support from white benefactors and to expand her efforts in the public relations. Mary had such charisma and personality that she continued to draw support from the black community as well as wealthy whites in the Daytona area. She was a prolific letter writer, writing to rich and famous people for support and getting letters on the editorial page in the Daytona *News Journal* as well as the New York *Times*. She continued to have the choir perform at the beachside hotels where she would have opportunity to ask for donations and meet benefactors. Fruitcakes and sweet potato pies were items that students prepared and sold to bring in money for the school. She continued to recruit outstanding and wealthy individuals to serve on the Board of Trustees. For example, Mrs. Patricia Bennett talked about her father, Mr. Thompson, who was a descendant of one of the town's founding fathers and a well-respected businessman. He and others like him were recruited by Mary to serve as trustees. Bennett commented that Mary was remarkable in that she had such a keen mind and superb business sense at a time when women, especially black women, were not recognized as being important in society. Mrs. Thompson, like many other wealthy white women in the community, listened to Mary's petitions and donated items such as dishes, clothing and other items that could be used by the school. Mary's charisma, perseverance, and faith kept the school going and growing.

On the Fourth of July, 1913, Mary went for a rare ride to the beach with friends. The moon was bright and it was a lovely evening. Somehow, she started to step out on the sand as the car was slowly rolling to a stop; she fell onto the hard sand and broke her left arm. Returning to the McLeod Hospital, the doctor discovered a complicated break at the elbow that would require special treatment. Mr. Gamble sent money and Mr. White arranged for her to be taken to Christ Hospital in Cincinnati, Ohio. She underwent painful therapy but also had a few weeks of rest, and returned to Daytona fully recovered. Mr. Gamble and Mr. White also purchased three small lots with a cottage behind Faith Hall. This became her "Retreat," and this home was her official residence until her death.

Dr. Bethune and students in front of White Hall in the 1940's.

This is Dr. Bethune's desk in her study at the Retreat.

Expansion continued as the school's enrollment grew. Mary convinced Mr. Mellour to purchase twelve acres of land across from Faith Hall when the Board of Trustees balked at such expenditure. This land was soon turned into additional farmland for raising vegetables, fruit, and chickens. Each student was assigned a plot of ground, and she could grow whatever she wanted in her own little garden. Frank Taylor used the horse, Queen, to plow some of the field and Mr. White personally purchased a mule named Bush to do work such as pulling the wooden pole around the sugar cane mill to press the cane and produce syrup. Tuskegee Institute sent a gift of two hogs. The advisory board member donated a cow, which was named Ridgewood, after the women's hometown in New Jersey. The school was prospering and the students were not only learning agriculture but also contributing by supplying produce for food. Produce was also sold to the community to supplement funds.

The school in 1915 had grades one through twelve, with the last two years focused on teaching students a trade. Tirelessly Mary continued to expand the school, travel to get funds and develop benefactors, and expand services to the community. She promoted integration at a time when no other place in the South permitted it. She began Temperance meetings every Sunday at 3:00 p.m., and all members of the community would come to hear famous speakers she invited, and share ideas with fellow community members. Ushers placed people, white or black, wherever there was a vacant seat. Everyone sat together. Students performed at these meetings, and the student concert chorale was an important fundraising tool. Soon, students had broadened their venues to include tours around Florida and beyond.

The wealthy white visitors were still placed in an area closer to the stage, but other concert goers, black and white, were seated on a "first come" basis without regard to race. According to one story, a wealthy white individual came to the door and asked where was the area for white people to sit. One of the students sought out Mary and told her that this person wanted special seating. Her reply was that color did not matter in her chapel—people could sit where there was an available seat or not sit at all. Mary McLeod Bethune's personality and prestige were so strong that few questioned the fact that these Sunday community meetings were integrated at a time where few places in the South would allow the races to mix.

Students performed in the school chapel in Faith Hall, and the collection basket was always passed around. When Dr. Bethune walked in, the student body would stand and sing "Let Me Call You Sweetheart," which was their tribute to her. This became the school tradition. One former football player recalled that this custom was still in place even when she was in her late 70s.

Cy McClairen, a student and football player in the early 1950s, remembered the first time he saw her. Dr. Bethune was often absent on political trips and her visits to campus were rare. He was in the chapel for a required Sunday program when suddenly the speaker stopped and everyone stood up. As a little woman using a cane walked down the aisle with the dignity of a queen, the students broke out in song. Being a new student, he had to ask someone what was happening. He still remembers with awe how she commanded the respect and reverence from all who were in the chapel that day. When she got on stage and began to speak, he was overwhelmed at her powerful presence and speaking ability. "I had been about to fall asleep before her arrival," he recalled, "but now I was wide awake and totally interested as she captured the crowd with her magnetism." Sunday Community Meetings were a tradition, which continued until Mary's death.

Chapter 3

Mary the Politician

"Enter to learn; depart to serve."

M ary worked hard to keep the school solvent and the school's archives contain some of the many letters she wrote to famous people and publications asking for support. The reputation of the school grew, as did Mary's reputation. In addition to her work on behalf of the school, she soon became involved with improving the status of black women through political and charitable organizations.

In 1914, Mary made her first trip to Washington after the outbreak of World War I. The leadership of the Red Cross, the nation's premier charitable organization, faced a dilemma—should Negroes be permitted to participate, or should they continue to be excluded from participation in this worthy organization? Mary had met Senator Frederic Walcott when he was on vacation at the Ormond Hotel. He had been impressed with her speech, talked with her after the students' program, and joined the Institute's Board of Trustees. He recommended her to Mr. S. J. Peabody, who was a friend of Vice President Thomas Marshall and who served as the chairman of the Red Cross. Mary was asked to take a train to Washington to present her views at a meeting that was focused on the Red Cross' policies. Hurriedly, she got some friends who were seamstresses to help her alter some contributed skirts and blouses so that she would have suitable clothing for a visit to the capital. Despite her pieced together wardrobe, she presented ideas so well and so convincingly that she was asked to travel with three white women for two weeks to Maryland, Pennsylvania, and Virginia to speak on support of Negroes working with the Red Cross. Finally, the decision was made that the Red Cross would be integrated.

Mary was a leader in getting black women involved with the Red Cross and the war effort in Florida. She was elected president of the Florida Federation of Colored Women's Clubs in 1917 and promptly began reorganizing this group and expanding membership. Under her leadership, the FFCWC opened a home for delinquent girls in Ocala, organized support for the military fighting in World War I and actively campaigned for passage of the Nineteenth Amendment to give women the right to vote.

In 1917, she also began to organize black women to push for voter registration of blacks. Not everyone in the community appreciated the idea of integration and the right of African-Americans to vote. Disbanded in the 1870s, the Ku Klux Klan re-formed in 1915. Pushing a program to deny the right to vote to anyone who was not white, Protestant and Anglo-Saxon, the Klan also conducted a vociferous and frequently violent campaign against African-Americans, Catholics, Jews and immigrants who sought to exercise political, social and economic rights. Anyone who was not white and native born, the Klan argued, was inferior and did not deserve to be considered equal in any arena. The KKK in Daytona became more visible when a controversial local election for mayor drew near. The KKK-backed candidate was running against a prohibitionist who supported the building of a black high school as well as better streets, lights, and sewage for the black neighborhoods. Mary was organizing the black ministers and other influential blacks to encourage the African-American community to register to vote and to participate in the election.

One evening, Father Doyle from St. Paul's Catholic Church came to Faith Hall where a meeting was being held. He had been a supporter of the school and of Mary's efforts since she started her work in Daytona. He warned the group that the KKK was planning activities the night before the election to terrorize the blacks and the Catholics in the town. He could not give specifics about the plan, but told all those present to be on their guard. Threats to her life did not discourage Dr. Bethune and she continued her push for voter registration. Around ten o'clock the night before the election, some one hundred hooded Klan members marched down Second Avenue and through the black district. A trumpet blasted as the figures marched behind their leader, who carried a huge burning wooden cross. The Klan had darkened the street by turning off the street lamps, and they marched with flaming torches through the darkened black neighborhood to the school campus in an effort to terrify the locals.

Frank Taylor was a plumber who lived near the school and worked evenings as the night watchman. He had his rifle over his shoulder and faced the Klansman when they approached the gate in the fence that surrounded the school. They ordered Frank to open the gate, which he did. The Klansmen encircled Faith Hall where the students and faculty were gathered. Dr. Bethune had ordered all lights off in the building, but then turned on the outside yard lights so that the Klansmen would be clearly illuminated and would lose some of the impact of their frightening appearance under the bright lights. However, one of the children looking through the window panicked and began to scream and others followed suit. Then one girl's voice began to sing the hymn "Be not dismayed whate'er be; God will take care of you." The other girls joined in and gradually the screams of panic were replaced by the voices of the students singing this hymn. The Klan finally left as they realized their effort to intimidate the women and children had failed; no one was harmed.

The election was held with the black voters standing on the street for hours while the white voters cast their ballots first. At the end of the day, Mary and the other blacks finally got to vote. Lined up for five blocks at 7:00 p.m., they continued to cast their votes until 1:00 a.m. The Klan candidate was defeated, and the more progressive candidate was elected.

Mary continued in her organization of the black women when she founded the Southeastern Federation of Negro Women in 1920. Soon she had a well-organized group of two thousand clubs in twelve states. The use of tiers from local to state to national levels allowed for better communications and organized activities. Great efforts were made to communicate and work with white women and the National Council of Women.

The school continued to expand. For years, one elderly woman named Flora Curtis was a steady customer for the fruits and vegetables grown by the school's students, who took special care to provide her with the very best produce. When she died in 1920, she left $80,000 to the Institute, asking only that fresh flowers be kept on her grave in Buffalo, New York. With continued support from Mr. Gamble, the yearly endowment left after Mr. White died in 1914, and this endowment from Mrs. Curtis, Mary had enough money in 1923 to build Curtis Hall, a dormitory on the campus of the Daytona Normal and Industrial Institute.

Mary also solicited support from the philanthropist S. J. Peabody, who had donated funds for the Peabody Auditorium in Daytona. He helped students with scholarships to Talladega College, donated the equipment for the auditorium when White Hall was built, and bequeathed $10,000 in his will for the institute. A trustee, Harrison Rhodes, became active as an assistant financial director and he wrote a letter to the Carnegie Foundation asking for a grant for books. When the Foundation responded positively, a room in Faith Hall was transformed into a library, and the public was given free access to the collection.

Rhodes persuaded Mrs. Orme Wilson of the Astor family to have Mary come to New York and speak in the spring to her wealthy friends. Mary gave a description of the school, its students and its programs to about fifty guests, including the Vanderbilts, Pierponts, and Guggenheims.

One woman, Mrs. Frank Chapman, who resided in Ormond Beach in the winter, was so impressed with Bethune's presentation about the school, she planned a program at the ballroom of the Ormond Hotel and invited many influential friends to attend. Mary had a few of the girls with her who sang and recited readings for the audience. One of these young girls, Maude Ella Purcell, so impressed John D. Rockefeller that he donated one thousand dol-

This building was dedicated in 1942 to Harrison Garfield Rhodes who had established the first library on campus and had arranged for his estate to be given to the college.

lars for her education, and Mrs. Ann Pierpont Luquer sponsored the child through high school and college. Maude continued on to postgraduate school at Boston College. Mr. Rockefeller enjoyed having the students come to his Casements mansion, which he built near the Ormond Hotel on the river. He was famous for giving out dimes to children, and he often gave dimes to the students when he visited campus. Mary became friends with his son John D. Rockefeller, Jr. Their conversations about education and the activities at the Institute impressed him, and later he was helpful in authorizing grant money for the Institute from the General Education Board.

Harrison Rhodes continued to help with developing the curriculum and with financial advice until his death in 1922. He left his estate to his sister with instructions that the income would transfer to the college at her death, and the Harrison Rhodes Building on campus is dedicated to his memory.

Black women continued to organize under Mary's leadership, and, in 1924, Mary was elected president of the National Association of Colored Women. At a convention held in Memphis, Dr. Will Alexander talked to the group about the segregation of troops during the First World War and his work to bring blacks and whites together to discuss the attitudes and conditions of a segregated military even while all Americans were fighting for the same cause. At this conference, one-third of the attendees were white women who had been invited to listen and share ideas. This meeting was the first time that black and white women discussed common problems in a public forum and they realized that the goal of the various women's groups and clubs — a better world for children — was similar. Mary also suggested that the NACW develop a national headquarters where files and records could be stored and where a center for communications could be established.

In 1926, she addressed the Fifteenth Biennial Convention of the National Association of Colored Women in Oakland, California. Her three main issues were conditions within the race, the national racial environment, and the world conditions that influenced the present and future of people of color in general. She encouraged the women to work for increased minority participation in the fields of art, science, and education. She asked that all blacks work together in harmony for the common good of all. She also encouraged protests against any denial of the equal share of opportunities, liberty, and protection as Americans, and she urged a link between peoples of color throughout the world. Her vision was a world gathering of colored women who would carry "the torch of freedom, equal rights, and human love — holding it high and brightening the world with rays of justice, tolerance and faithful service in God's name."

In 1927, Mary was overjoyed when she got the opportunity to go to Europe. Dr. Wilberforce Williams, a surgeon from Chicago, was organizing a group to tour nine countries. He had taken groups to Europe before and Mary felt it would a great experience to tour nine European countries with seasoned travelers. Mary did not have the income for such a trip, but her friends donated money for the travel as well as gifts of luggage so that she could travel in style. Ironically, Mary, who prided herself on never being late, was delayed when the train coming from Daytona encountered difficulties. Mary phoned her friends in New York, and asked them to try to hold the boat until she arrived. She arrived at the pier thirty minutes late and walked onto the ship while passengers wondered who this woman was whose friends had such influence that the ship was held up for her arrival. The *S.S. Olympic* sailed on May 28, and Mary had four months to see Europe.

Her first stop was London where she went to Westminster Abbey and had tea with the Lord Mayor of London. A friend from America who was studying music in England introduced her to many places and people, including Lady Nancy Astor who held a lavish garden party for Mary at the Astor country home. Mary went to Scotland where she visited the International House of Women and then attended a tea party given in her honor by Lady Edith McLeod. Her skin color was never a problem as the Europeans had no history of segregation, and her fame as an educator and founder of a school earned respect from all whom she met. Only one time did she report an incident of racism in the British Isles. She was eating at a restaurant in a small English town when she heard a group of white Americans protest that they were not used to eating with Negroes. The proprietor simply told the Americans that he was unaware of American customs, but in his restaurant, the customer gets what he pays for. That ended the discussion.

Heading on to Paris, Mary spent hours at the Louvre and the Luxembourg Galleries. Not truly an academic with a background in the classics, Mary readily absorbed the history, art, and culture of these countries. She saw the historical sites throughout Paris, and also bought herself two Parisian gowns. Now at the age of fifty-two, Mary had acquired a taste for fashion and she was always corseted, tastefully dressed in conservative colors, and adorned with simple jewelry such as the simulated pearls she most often wore. She took great pride in neatness, graceful bearing, and straight posture.

Mary toured Germany and in Belgium was impressed with the simplicity of the royal family who rode the tram and sold apples for charity. She visited The Hague and then Berne, Switzerland. It was here that she saw a hillside filled with roses of every shade and hue, which she called her international garden, representing the human race as every color and shade together created an overall design of beauty. Mary wrote, "Roses of every color! And in the midst of the garden, I saw a great big Black Velvet Rose. I never saw a Black Velvet Rose before, and I said to myself, 'Oh! This is the great interracial garden; this is the garden where we have people of all colors, all classes, all creeds. People, every single one of them, getting their full chance to become the best they can become...This shall always be before me as a great Interracial Garden where men and women of all tongues, all nations, all creeds, all classes blend together helping to send out sunshine and love and peace and brotherhood that make a better world in which to live.'"

In Switzerland, Mary was given an alpenstock to use for climbing the hills. She found that she loved carrying and twirling this cane and this began a hobby of collecting canes from notable people. She carried a cane as her personal trademark, not really needing one, but enjoying the impression she made so much it became a part of her fashion style. She traveled on to see the wonders of Italy, receiving a special benediction from Pope Pius XI. She toured Genoa, observed gamblers in Monte Carlo, and finally sailed from Cherbourg on August 28 to return to the States. It had been a wonderful experience, which also made her understand the accomplishments of women in these other countries. She returned with a new dedication and a determination to convince American black women that they too were equal to and as capable as women worldwide.

Later in 1927, Mary was invited to attend a special luncheon at the home of

Mrs. Franklin Roosevelt in New York City. This was a meeting of representatives of the National Council of Women and Mary was the only Negro among the thirty-five guests. There was a moment of awkwardness, when some of the Southern women seemed hesitant about the seating arrangements. Mrs. Sara Delano Roosevelt solved the situation by taking Mary's arm and leading her to the seat at the right of the hostess, Eleanor Roosevelt. From that day, Mary became a close friend of Sara and Eleanor Roosevelt, friendships that endured until Mary died. As the president of the NCNW and a friend of the Roosevelt women, she was able to voice the concerns of black women on a national level, especially during the Roosevelt administration

The school's enrollment continued to expand and with a larger student body, the demand for more financial support kept apace. Mary was weary with the constant need for fundraising, despite the generous support of individuals on the Board of Trustees. Dr. Bethune sought a permanent source of income that would ensure the stable operation of the school without being solely dependent on her ability to raise funds. Other avenues of funding had to be found.

She did not want to ask for state funds because the state would demand that she relinquish control of the school. She simply could not allow that. She appealed to the Presbyterian Church Board in Pittsburgh, but was told no funds were available. The Roman Catholic Church, which had always supported her efforts, was another possible underwriter, but she knew that if the church took over, the Institute would become a Catholic school. She wanted it to remain nondenominational and independent. Permanent funding for the school looked to be just another unfulfilled desire. But, as had happened so often in the past, just when things appeared to be the darkest, a miracle happened.

Dr. G. Garland Penn proposed that she could merge with a small school for Negro boys that had been founded in Jacksonville in 1872 by Alfred Cookman, a white abolitionist. The Cookman Institute had been the first school for black boys in the state, but it was declining as other schools arose in Jacksonville. Affiliated with the Methodist Church, Penn proposed that this school would be merged with the Institute and that the Methodist Church would provide background financial security. What made the proposed arrangement different for the other religious affiliation was that the Methodist Church would grant Mary the freedom to control school policies and programs. Thus in April 1923, a new entity emerged as the Bethune-Cookman Collegiate Institute. Finally Mary had some financial security for her school, but it became coeducational, a fact that she would attempt to reverse ten years later. When she urged the Board of Trustees to return the school to a female only institution, the board responded that the young men would stay. The school was now a high school and junior college and lower grades had been eliminated. The school had 135 students and a debt of $22,000. Mary continued her efforts to raise funds for the school while her political involvement in national affairs grew.

By 1928, the women's organization she had founded was thriving and Mary announced the creation of a national headquarters in Washington, D.C. She hoped this headquarters would become a source of inspiration for blacks. The National Association of Colored Women's Headquarters was dedicated on July 28, 1928, at Twelfth and O Streets. At the end of her speech, she read the following poem:

> If you can't be a pine on top of the hill,
> Be a scrub in the valley;
> But be the best little scrub
> That grows by the till.
> Be a bush, if you can't be a tree.
> If you can't be a tree, be a bit of the grass.
> And some highway the happier make.
> If you can't be a muskie, just be a bass,
> But be the liveliest bass in the lake.
>
> We can't all be captains; we've got to be crew,
> There's plenty of work for us here.
> There's a bit work to do and a lesser;
> But our task is the one that is near.
> If you can't be a highway, just be a trail,
> If you can't be a sun, be a star.
> It's not in your size that you win or lose,
> Be the best of what ever you are!

In 1928, Mary established her first White House connection when Calvin Coolidge sponsored the Child Welfare Conference and asked her to attend. She was now considered one of the most influential black women in the country. For this second visit to Washington, she first went to New York and outfitted herself with new clothes, including a marten fur piece. She was the only Negro in the group to meet President Coolidge in the East Room of the White House. Without a smile, the President shook hands with each of the one hundred women and then left the room, leaving them to their meeting. This conference of educators and experts discussed ways to improve conditions for children and to keep the public informed about the work. Mary's task was to return to Florida and communicate to others what she had learned. Under President Herbert Hoover, the National Commission for Child Welfare continued and Mary was considered the Commission's expert on Negro education. Grants were made available for Negro institutions, and Mary was able to build a Science Hall and to replace Faith Hall with a brick edifice with dining hall and kitchen at her school in Daytona.

Florida was devastated by a hurricane in 1928, which hit especially hard in the southeast section of the state. Mary went with a group of women to survey the damage and immediately began organizing the Negro groups to address the needs. She wrote a letter asking for donation of supplies and funds as well as workers to clean up and rebuild. Her moving narrative described one brave Negro who saved eighteen people including white women. Another woman who was trying to swim across rushing waters with a child in one arm was attacked by an alligator, which bit off her other arm. She rescued the child nevertheless.

Mary also noted that the Seminole Indians living in the Everglades suddenly packed up and headed inland many days before the storm hit, telling all whom they met to follow them because, "Indian no fool. Going to dry land. Big water coming." People ignored the warning and perished while the Indians were all safe in the higher inland area they had sought. Daytona had only minor storm damage and Mary made the college a center for donations. She also helped to organize other sites in southern Florida, working with the Red Cross to meet the needs of the people. Schools were not able to meet that year along the southern tip of Florida. Times were very hard especially since a storm had hit Miami two years earlier, which exacerbated the financial disasters caused by the building boom collapse of 1926. The storm only added more burdens to those left homeless and distraught by the earlier catastrophes.

In Daytona, Mary kept the reins on her school although more of her time was now spent traveling or in Washington. In 1929, the school had 235 students and 25 faculty members. The graduating class boasted thirty high school diplomas, thirteen junior college certificates, three music degrees, and twenty business and home economics degrees. The college budget that year showed an income of $98,483 and disbursements of $96, 483, with about $3000 in cash and savings. Mary continued to promote the college and focused on the goals of the education and training of students, the development of a sympathetic attitude, the value of labor and industry, idealism, courage and faith. Her example of faith was a farmwoman in the South who gathered a group together to pray for rain in the midst of a long drought. As the group prayed, the rain began to fall in torrents. She always concluded her example with the words, "Following the glorious thanksgiving, farmer folk made ready to go home, but alas, the blessed rain prevented their venturing out—all but one little girl. 'I brought my umbrella,' she said, 'for I knew if we prayed for rain, it would come.' Hers was the vow of Faith."

The National Association of Colored Women held their 1930 convention in Los Angeles. Mary had always kept up correspondence with her benefactor,

Mary Chrisman, who had given her the scholarship that allowed Mary to attend school. Miss Chrisman was retired and living in Los Angeles, and they had their first and only reunion. As president of the NACW, Mary arranged for Miss Chrisman to sit at the head table as her guest of honor. Mary gave a rousing speech to the hundreds of women gathered, women who represented a variety of races including Chinese, Indians, and Mexicans. She emphasized the need for unity and organization among all women. Like a small mustard seed, she told them, their efforts could grow into the huge mustard tree with great branches. Mary also gave a tribute at the end to her guest, Miss Chrisman, whose sacrifice had enabled Mary to become a leader. As Mary accepted a huge bouquet of white rosebuds, she dedicated the flowers to Miss Chrisman. A few months later, Miss Chrisman died, never having been well enough to visit Daytona and see the Institute that was a result of her investment in Mary.

Chapter 4

Presidential Advisor Role

"Seek to be an artist: cease to be a drudge."

Mary was now famous. In 1931, she was listed as number ten among the fifty most outstanding living American women. However, it was at this time that her health problems became more serious. Having asthma and allergies, her health was often an obstacle she faced as she went about her work, but one that she fought constantly to overcome. Throughout her life, she had suffered with occasional asthma, but now she was struck by incapacitating respiratory difficulties that required surgery. Friends arranged for her to have a sinus operation at the Cleveland Clinic, followed by a few weeks of recuperation in Bermuda. She returned rested and recovered. The surgery on her sinuses seemed to help the chronic infections she suffered and she went back to work with a renewed passion.

Franklin Roosevelt was elected president in 1932 and his New Deal policies included appointing Negro advisors for various government agencies. The country was still in the depths of the depression and over one-fourth of the nation's youths, some five million in number, were unemployed and uneducated. Blacks in the South were especially hard hit as scarce jobs were given to the whites and black schools remained under-funded. Juvenile delinquency was on the rise and so, too, was the number of young men who took to the road in search of work. President Roosevelt started the National Youth Administration in 1934 to address these problems.

Bethune-Cookman Institute continued to expand its campus with a science hall and a renovated Faith Hall in 1935. At this time, college finances became a concern. Many of the institution's original supporters had died and the money from the White Foundation was reduced. Besides her political efforts, Mary never forgot her first loyalty was to the Institute and she was always searching for funds for her school. The more her involvement with activities in Washington grew, the more she left Dean James A. Bond to run the school. But despite a busy political agenda, Dr. Bethune continued to pursue funding for the Institute. It was her cross to bear throughout her lifetime.

On June 23, 1935, Mary was awarded the Spingarn Award from the National Association for the Advancement of Colored People for her service to her race. Assistant Secretary of the Treasury Josephine Roche presented the medal to her, and after she heard Mary's impressive speech of acceptance, they discussed their ideas. Secretary Roche recommended Mary for the Advisory Board for the National Youth Administration. Mary became a representative for Florida and also a member of a special consultants group within the agency.

She met President Roosevelt in the White House at a meeting to discuss the progress of the NYA. Mary gave an emotional report about what NYA meant to black youths and described the Negro situation of poverty and depression within the larger context of the Depression. She pleaded with the president to exert his influence and open doors for Negroes to show them that somebody in administration cared. The president was openly moved by her speech, and, grasping her hands in both of his, assured her that he would do his best. Afterward, Aubrey Williams, the Director of NYA who was a close friend of the President, thanked her for her inspirational report. A week later Mary received a letter from the President requesting a meeting. Aubrey Williams informed her that the President had been so impressed with Mary's appeal that he set up a new Office of Minority

Shown with the Capitol Building in the background, Dr. Bethune was advisor for four presidents and played a major political role as a representative for minorities.

Affairs within the NYA, and that he wanted her to be the administrator. Mary's first reaction was to decline because she was still engaged in the operations of her school, which was now called Bethune-Cookman College. Williams pointed out that she would be the first Negro woman in history to hold a federal post, a distinction that would immeasurably aid the cause of African-Americans. She finally agreed to accept. Roosevelt met with her later. He had total faith in her ability, he said, because she had her feet not only on the ground, but also in the deep, plowed soil.

Mary began to hold informal meetings at her house with influential black men who were government advisors. She believed they needed to collaborate and work to get even more knowledgeable blacks into government. The number who came to these meetings grew as well as the qualified Negroes who were being appointed as consultants. The group would discuss individuals for positions, and Mary, who now had open access to the President, would give him the group's suggestions. With her great leadership skill, she was able to gather these men and keep them focused on their objectives. The group would not meet if Mary was unable to be there to convene the meeting. This group became known as the Black Cabinet.

Then Mary had the idea to hold a national conference of Negro leadership that would bring together representatives from all fields and all sections of the country. This three day Conference on Civil Liberties met on January 6, 1937, in the Department of Labor auditorium. The hundred or so delegates discussed the varied problems of Negroes across the country and developed recommendations that became known as the "Blue Book" of this first conference. Mary went to President Roosevelt and eloquently told him about the conference proceedings as she gave him a copy of the "Blue Book." The "Blue Book" was distributed to the Cabinet, administrative heads, and all members of Congress. Mary also interceded for the Negro press and helped the first black reporter get credentials and admittance to the Presidential press conferences.

Mary had always been a Republican because it was tradition among Negroes to follow the party of Abraham Lincoln. However, she switched to the Democratic Party because she believed in what Roosevelt was trying to do. She believed the Democratic Party now better represented the needs and concerns of Negroes. Her friendship with President Roosevelt deepened as his respect for her opinions and ideas grew. He proved to be a true humanitarian who was concerned about the common people. The president's concern for people was summed up in a single instance. When an old farmer from Mississippi used his last coins to call the President directly to ask for help because he was losing his farm because of debt. After Mary and the president discussed the farmer's dilemma, he sent an official by plane to talk to the sheriff and work out a plan to save the old farmer and his wife from eviction. Although many wealthy people disliked President Roosevelt and his New Deal policies, to Mary and those like her who represented the poorer classes, he was a hero. As administrator in the NYA, Mary traveled throughout all regions of the South to meet people and hear their stories.

Mary received an invitation to President Roosevelt's second inauguration.

A ticket collector asked for her ticket and recommended that she sit far in the back in a reserved section. Mary simply walked past him and moved to the front row close to the Presidential stand. Hers was one of the very few black faces at this ceremony and at most gatherings in Washington. She was proud of her many accomplishments, but in her diary she wrote after attending tea at the Executive Mansion, "While I felt very much at home, I looked about me longingly for other dark faces. In all that great group, I felt a sense of being quite alone...Then I thought how vitally important it was that I be here, to help those others get used to seeing us in high places."

Mary's title was changed to director of the Negro Affairs, an important position in the National Youth Administration. The goal of the NYA was similar to that of the Civilian Conservation Corps, which was to put young men to work on building of parks, bridges, roads, and other restoration and reclamation projects. The NYA provided three programs: Works, Student Aid, and Placement. Young men and women between the ages of sixteen and twenty-four received job training, education and guidance. The motto was "To earn and to learn." Youths were paid fourteen dollars a month on work projects. The work experience varied from clerical and research to farming and home management. She went around the country encouraging the Negro youths to join; she also educated the public about the program and worked with directors to ensure that the programs were running efficiently. She constantly instilled pride in the black youths by urging them to work hard and learn all they could from the NYA experience. In 1937, these young people helped with the relief efforts in areas heavily flooded when rivers overran their banks. Another project they were involved in was reconstructing the home and property of Frederick Douglas in Washington, D.C. that had been purchased by the National Council of Negro Women as a memorial. All youth were paid the same for whatever project they worked on, including choral and art activities.

Under the student program, aid was administered equally to blacks and whites. More than 150,000 Negro youths earned high school degrees while over 60,000 were given a chance to attend college or graduate school. Mary also fought for funding for Negro youths who lived in southern states where they were denied admittance to state-funded graduate schools, in order to ensure that these students could attend Negro universities like Howard or Fisk, or go north to other schools that were not segregated. In 1937, Congress wanted to tighten the NYA's budget, so the $100,000 earmarked for the graduate school program funding was to be cut. Mary made an appointment with President Roosevelt the same day she heard about the funding cut. She was so emotional when she spoke to him about the importance of this funding that she suddenly realized she was waving her finger right in his face and caught herself in embarrassment. She apologized for being so emotional. He just smiled, said he understood and promised he would see what he could do. A week later, the cuts to NYA were eliminated and full funding was restored.

Within two years, 375 of the NYA funded students had earned graduate degrees with honors from Pennsylvania institutes, proving that the program was successful. Mary spent the next eight years traveling and serving as a clearinghouse for projects and communication between the different agencies. In one year, she traveled to twenty-one states overseeing sixty-nine centers, or some forty thousand miles in all. She held forty-one meetings, opened six new centers, and gave three commencement speeches.

Eleanor Roosevelt and Mary had become close friends, and that friendship gave Mary greater political clout. She and Mrs. Roosevelt shared the same ideas and goals. This friendship was helpful as Mary expanded her activity and influence. When the mayor of Daytona and community leaders came to her for support of a project to clean up the shanties in the Negro section, Mary called Mrs. Roosevelt and told her she needed an allocation of a half-million dollars. On June 25, 1939, ground was broken for the Pine Haven Housing Project, which consisted of cottages, recreation areas, and a swimming pool constructed by the NYA.

Dr. Bethune and Eleanor Roosevelt were very close friends and allies in political activities.

Secretary of Agriculture Henry Wallace asked Dr. Bethune to serve on a national committee created to examine the conditions of black tenant farmers in the South. During the committee's hearings on the problem, one large landowner from Mississippi declared that his ninety "coons" were happy and did not need to be disturbed by issues of sanitation, schools, and housing. When he reported that they were "good niggers" just the way they were, Mary found the eyes of all committee members embarrassingly turned her way. She controlled her anger and made no response to his comments. Secretary Wallace later wrote Mary a note of thanks, extolling her work to bring respect for Negro women and stating his wish that African-Americans had more leaders like her.

During this same period, she pushed the National Council of Negro Women, which she had founded in 1935, as a way to better organize the Negro women on a national level, serve as a clearing house for Federal departments dealing with women and children, and finally expand into an international program for women worldwide. The Council expanded rapidly, and the group decided they had to have a separate headquarters building instead of using an office located at Mary's residence in Washington. In an

39

effort to find money for this endeavor, Mary visited Marshall Field III in Chicago.

He had given $11 million to the Field Foundation in an effort to find solutions for the problems the nation faced in the relations between whites and blacks. Mary asked him for a donation of ten thousand dollars for the Council headquarters. He replied that he had faith in her and would mail her the check. She asked if she could carry it back with her to inspire the staff and members. He laughed and wrote out the check immediately, chuckling that no one could have told him he would be giving away that amount of money so quickly.

This money helped to establish the Women's Council Headquarters located on Vermont Ave. in Washington, D.C. Under her leadership, the headquarters became a center for archives of historical books, letters, medals, and other items that highlighted the achievements of Negro women and of black culture in general. The council started publication of a quarterly magazine, *The Aframerican Woman's Journal*, in 1940, which later became the magazine *Women United* in 1949. A monthly *Telefact* flyer kept members apprised of important events and other valuable general information about individuals and programs. Mary also began a regular column in the Pittsburgh *Courier* called "Day By Day" and a column in the Chicago *Defender* called "Mary McLeod Bethune." These publications helped create a public awareness of problems faced by minorities worldwide. When Mary retired as its president in 1949, the council had 850,000 members, twenty-one affiliated organizations and ninety local chapters.

On January 12, 1939, Mary convened the second National Negro Conference, which was held in the Department of Labor Auditorium. More than one thousand delegates were in attendance and the focus of the conference was to evaluate the progress made over the last two years on the recommendations of the first conference on civil liberties. Mary announced that she represented the Federal Council of Negro Affairs, a group of blacks who held strategic positions in government. She asked Lester B. Granger, Executive Secretary of the National Urban League, to become chairman of the Findings Committee. His job was to attend every general meeting and every special committee meeting at the conference, and write up a summary report within a few weeks. Mr. Granger said, "Mrs. Bethune had the most marvelous gift of affecting feminine helplessness in order to attain her ends with masculine ruthlessness. She knew how to pull all the stops in her beautiful speaking voice in order to achieve the exact result desired from a large audience or one or two listeners."

At one time, when the group broke into argument over an issue, Mary, with the theatrical flair of an experienced actress, took over the meeting. She stood up and declared she was an old, confused woman who asked for common sense instead of the bickering. With that, she got the group back on track. Although she was now sixty-four years old, no one could ever accuse her of being old and confused.

The conference compiled reports and made recommendations. Among the many recommendations was a demand for group medical plans, followed by a plea for compulsory insurance to lower the cost of medical care. Other recommendations included a desire for better birth control education, a request for the appointment of an African-American to the Red Cross Board, the condemnation of discrimination in government appointments and promotions, and opposition of any federal housing programs that promoted or allowed segregation. The conference also endorsed use of fingerprints instead of photographs to verify identity of applicants for civil service positions, which the members felt would discourage racial discrimination in filling these jobs. The Civil Service Commission immediately opposed this recommendation by claiming fingerprints were too expensive to collect and evaluate. Bethune and two representatives from the conference met with Roosevelt to give him a summary of findings and recommendations made by the delegates to the conference. The next day Mary received a personal letter from the president thanking her for her efforts and encouraging her to continue working for the improvement and inclusion of blacks in American society.

Mary and Eleanor Roosevelt were close friends united by similar interests and common causes. Mrs. Roosevelt accepted an invitation to visit Bethune-Cookman College in February 1940. Three representatives of the nonsectarian Tourist Church in Daytona approached Bethune and told her that wealthy residents of Daytona were against Mrs. Roosevelt's visit. Mary refused to be intimidated by this delegation, but she did arrange for Mrs. Roosevelt to stay at the Princess Issena Hotel since the local white community would be shocked if the white wife of the president should stay on the black college campus. That was all she was willing to do to accommodate their feelings. She certainly would not retract the invitation to visit the college.

Dr. Bethune and Eleanor Roosevelt were very close friends and allies in political activities. Mrs. Roosevelt made several visits to the campus, but stayed at a hotel on beachside due to the segregation rules of the day.

A large crowd was expected to hear Mrs. Roosevelt make a short speech, and an outdoor platform was built near White Hall. Just as she began to speak, raindrops began to fall. Mary immediately took the podium and declared that the black community had been waiting for such an event for thirty-five years and that a little bit of rain would not stop this monumental occasion. The rain stopped and Mrs. Roosevelt gave her ten-minute speech to the outside crowd. When the rain resumed, the program was completed inside the auditorium. Mrs. Roosevelt was so impressed with the junior college and its students that, on her return to Washington, she helped Mary by sponsoring fundraising events with dignitaries and wealthy people in the city.

Built in 1916, White Hall, named after friend and supporter, Thomas White, was the first brick structure on campus.

The stress of her job and her increasingly poor health took a toll on Mary. Nearly sixty-five years old, she weighed two hundred pounds, and her asthma and breathing problems had worsened. Mrs. Roosevelt arranged for Mary to enter John Hopkins University where she was put on a diet and prepared for sinus surgery. After three weeks, she had rested and lost weight, so a white surgeon was called in to perform the surgery since John Hopkins would not allow black surgeons in the operating room. Mary insisted that two black surgeons be allowed to observe the procedure, and she was finally given her wish. After three more weeks, Mary had fully recovered and was released. John D. Rockefeller heard of her illness and sent her a check for one thousand dollars, which she immediately sent down to Daytona for the college.

Despite her fame, Mary continued to face discrimination on her travels around the United States. On a trip to North Carolina to speak to the NYA youths, she was told not to arrive too early at the hall or she would be asked to stay in the kitchen. On a train trip from Florida to Washington, she was referred to as "Auntie" by an elderly white ticket collector. She retorted,

White Hall Chapel. The chapel was the site of the Sunday Community Meetings.

"Which one of my sister's sons are you, James or John?" Another time Mary heard a small blond girl asking her mother loudly what a cook was doing traveling on the train with them, as the child only knew Negroes to be cooks or maids. People were not used to seeing a black woman riding trains to Hyde Park or staying as a guest at hotels. One cab driver was reluctant to give her a ride because he felt all black people were impudent and that she would rob him. She patiently explained to him who she was, what her job was and how she was a friend of the Roosevelts. She urged him not to stereotype all blacks based on his experiences with a few.

In 1941, Bethune-Cookman College was still facing financial problems. Although it now offered a four-year college degree program and had a growing enrollment, tuition never covered the entire expenses involved in keeping the institution going. Mary wrote both President and Mrs. Roosevelt for help in raising funds for the school. Her health was declining, she explained, and doctors told her she must cutback on her activities, resign as president of the college, or die. She submitted her resignation, recommending James Colston as her successor. Ironically, Mary's health improved somewhat, and in 1946, she became dissatisfied with the way Colston was running the school. She arranged his ouster and took control as president for one more year. In 1947, she resigned and Dr. Richard V. Moore took over as the president of the college.

Chapter 5

World War II

"If our people are to fight their way up out of bondage, we must arm them with the sword and the shield and the buckler of pride."

M ary Bethune had always followed an independent path in religion and politics. She had a deep faith in God, but never adhered to one particular religion or church, simply accepting them all. In politics, she was a registered Republican because most blacks still viewed that party as the party of the Great Emancipator, Abraham Lincoln. But she voted or supported candidates, regardless of the party, whom she felt were the best for poor blacks and whites. After meeting President Roosevelt and seeing the compassion and concern he had for blacks and poor in the country, she registered as a Democrat. She firmly believed in the social philosophy of the progressive New Deal Democrats and President Roosevelt.

In 1941 at the third National Negro Conference, Mary gave a speech and asked that African-Americans be given an equal opportunity to help defend the country. With the United States increasingly involved in aiding Great Britain in the war in Europe and likely to be drawn into the conflict directly, Negroes wanted to play a role in the nation's military if war came. "Despite the attitude of some employers in refusing to hire Negroes to perform needed, skilled services," she declared," and despite the denial of the same opportunities and courtesies to our youth in the armed forces of our country, we must not fail America and as Americans, we must not let America fail us." She strongly believed that blacks were entitled to participate in every aspect of American life, including the right to die in its defense.

Meanwhile the NYA was being carefully scrutinized to determine the effectiveness of the program. NYA youths were being trained in a variety of skills and then transferred to areas where war production jobs were available. The result was that Negro youths were given the experience of seeing different parts of the country and of working in industry. On the assembly lines around the country, some 400,000 young black men were contributing to the war effort. Despite this remarkable achievement, over two million were still unemployed.

After Pearl Harbor, a budget battle occurred in Congress over whether or not the NYA and Civilian Conservation Corps programs should be continued. Two Democrat senators, Harry S. Truman of Missouri and Walter F. George of Georgia, managed to save the NYA although the CCC program was abolished. With the country now at war, Mary was recruited to assist Lieutenant Colonel Oveta Hobby in selecting Negro women for Officers' Training School. Although a white southerner and a Texan, Colonel Hobby was unbiased and worked to support integration as much as possible under the Army regulations. Of the first 450 officer candidates, forty were to be Negroes. Of the eight companies to be trained, two were to be Negroes. However, segregation continued as the young black women were housed in separate barracks and not allowed to sit with

During the World War II, Dr. Bethune was active in supporting female as well as black participation in the military.

white trainees at meals. This policy was followed rigorously despite the fact that whites and blacks received the same training in mixed groups. Dr. Bethune voiced her disagreement with this policy, but such conditions of segregation continued throughout the war.

Mary was on the board of directors for the American Women's Voluntary Service, which supported the war effort through activities such as blood donations, campaigns, canteen staffing, and war bond sales. This group helped sponsor the International Women's Exposition held in Madison Square Garden, where it conducted a volunteer training workshop to encourage women of all ages to get involved in the war effort in some capacity.

Another organization that Mary participated in as a leading member was the Southern Conference for Human Welfare, which originated with Roosevelt's desire to learn why the South was so far behind the rest of the country in economic growth. A report commissioned by the National Emergency Council revealed a pattern of poverty, racial discrimination, segregation, and poor education, which was complicated by a reliance on the unproductive sharecropper system and absentee owners. The SCHW held its first meeting in Birmingham in 1938. Despite enjoying an inspirational first evening of speeches and prayers for social justice as an integrated group, the participants faced the harsh reality of the Jim Crow system the next morning when police arrived to enforce the state's policy of strict segregation. The Negro delegates were told to use the side doors and to sit in separate areas from the white participants. Faced with the reality of southern determination to enforce its customs, the group, which included the wife of the president of the United States, had no choice but to follow the law or face imprisonment for breaking it. People were suddenly very nervous and intimidated by the police who remained to make sure the "no mixing of races" laws were observed.

In order to bridge the artificial void among the delegates this action created, Mrs. Roosevelt moved her chair into the middle of the aisle between the two groups. While this small gesture did a great deal to reduce the tension created by the police, it did not completely erase the overwhelming presence of racism. The woman who introduced Mary as a speaker did so by simple calling her name, "Mary Bethune." This was in accord with the southern custom that blacks were never given a title nor honorifics of any kind.

There was a nervous silence at this breech in etiquette. Mary made her way to the podium and announced, "Madame Chairman, for the record I am Mrs. Mary McLeod Bethune. I wish to have this on record so that others will not accept the fact that this is 'Mary' speaking, but Mrs. Mary McLeod Bethune." Her imposing presence and unwillingness to accept this slight seemed to put the group at ease and the discussions that followed her talk were lively and focused. Although she was to be a featured participant in the program, that evening Mary faced the dilemma of entering the building through the alley door and having to sit in the area designated for Negroes. Aubrey Williams stepped forward when he saw her arrive and escorted her directly to the dais where Mrs. Roosevelt stood up and offered her own seat for Mary. Quickly, many of the members stood and offered their seats to Mrs. Roosevelt.

Based on the information presented and on the delegates' personal experiences with the Birmingham police, the conference reached the conclusion that the single greatest deterrent to prosperity in the South was the Jim Crow system of segregation that permeated every aspect of southern life.

In 1942, the group met in Nashville, where they had been assured that segregation would not be enforced within the meeting hall. However, Mary was told that she could not use the main elevator with the whites but instead had to take freight elevator. Mary decided to refuse this indignity and walked up the six floors to the hall, which led to an asthma attack later that evening. However, she was able to receive a special honor that she shared with Dr. Frank Graham from the University of North Carolina. She was the first Negro to be awarded the Thomas Jefferson Award from the Southern Conference for Human Welfare.

Her activities for civil rights and equality attracted the attention of the Federal Bureau of Investigation. She received a letter from Director of Personnel R. N. Barnett that the FBI had conducted an investigation of her. On August 31, 1942, he assured her that the FBI had not found any evidence of illegal or subversive activity. However, as the Southern Conference for Human Welfare continued with its advocacy for the right of workers to meet freely and organize for bargaining for better working conditions for all—blacks and whites—a fear of communism and the potential fro its spread the United States developed among political leaders of the nation. In the House of Representatives, a Committee on Un-American Activities was established. Texas Representative Martin Dies, chairman of this committee, publicly accused Mary of being a communist. This accusation created some stir across the country as newspaper editorials came to her defense. *The Churchman*, a publication of the Methodist Church, carried a statement by Bishop G. Bromley Oxnam, "To call Mrs. Bethune 'red' is not only most unfair to a most distinguished woman, but a sad commentary upon the work of a Congressional Committee." The Pittsburgh *Courier* and other papers throughout the country defended her in their editorials.

She finally gave a statement in her own defense:

"The absurdity of the charge inclined me, at first, to ignore it. I feel now, however, that I should brand the accusation for what it is—a malicious misstatement of the truth. I do not know Republican Dies. Because of his accusation, I am positive he does not know me. To those who know me I need no statement of denial. If Republican Dies sees fit to name me a Communist as a result of my outspoken belief in a true democracy, my incessant efforts in seeking for all Americans the Constitutionally guaranteed rights of full citizenship regardless of race, creed, or color, my endeavors to enlist the full cooperative strength of America in our victor efforts, then the names Mr. Dies chooses to apply are to me but tinkling cymbals and sounding brass. I shall continue along the straight true course I have followed through all these years, and I pray some Divine signal may sound in the mind of Mr. Dies that may awaken him to a realization that his accusations against loyal Americans will bring them but small discomfort, but can be of great comfort to our enemies."

Finally, on March 11, 1943, New York Republican Francis D. Culkin publicly stated that the committee did not say that Mary was a communist, but that there had been some communists on committees that she served on. "Her type of work is, in my judgment, the most effective antidote against communistic penetration among the Negroes." Mary continued her work with the Southern Conference for Human Welfare. In 1946, Mary gave a speech to the group, which was meeting in New Orleans. She urged three major changes in American society — lynching must be stopped, better wages must be paid to poor workers and the poll tax and other barriers to voting for blacks must be outlawed immediately. Her proposed changes were adopted by the SCHW as goals of the organization and some progress was made in achieving them during the ten years that the SCHW was in existence. The SCHW was disbanded in 1948 when the organized labor union movement became more powerful.

In addition to her continued involvement with various black women organizations, she was on the boards of several other organizations, such as the Planned Parenthood Federations of America, the National Sharecroppers Fund, the Friends of the Atlanta School of Social Work, Americans for Democratic Action, and the Harlem Division of the American Committee for Yugoslav Relief. Mary was involved in many groups and often lent her name in support of groups without thoroughly investigating their backgrounds. Despite the FBI investigation of her activities and the growing anti-communist fervor in the country, she continued to lend her name and support to various groups. She was a little more careful, however, in discovering more about the groups' activities and philosophies. For example, she withdrew her membership in and support of the Daughters of the Elks of America when she felt that a number of sponsors of the group "allowed themselves or their names to be associated with activities and organizations with whose methods and purposes I am unable to agree."

At this time, Mary decided to take up a local cause — that of providing Negroes in the Daytona area access to public beaches. Although the beaches had been open to all races in the early period of the town's existence, the KKK and segregationists in the 1920s had enacted segregation laws that prevented blacks from using the same beaches as whites. She purchased a large parcel of beachfront property twenty-three miles south of Daytona, which was subdivided and sold to blacks who wanted to live on beachside. The beach area was known as Bethune Beach and became the gathering point for blacks from all around the area. Soon the Welricha Motel opened to accommodate African-American visitors and eight hundred new owners bought and developed property. The social activities of the new residents made Bethune Beach a popular vacation spot. Until segregation ended in the 1960s, the Bethune Beach remained the only site where blacks could have access to the ocean.

Even with her many other activities, Mary became an active participant in the civil rights movement. She joined a picket line to support the two-year effort by the New Negro Alliance to boycott stores in Washington that refused to hire Negro clerks. The boycott ended when the stores agreed to employ Negro clerks. She supported a Bethune-Cookman graduate, Asa Philip Randolph, who organized a march on Washington for the Brotherhood of Sleeping Car Porters. However, President Roosevelt convinced the group to hold up the march and issued an executive order on June 25, 1941, which created the Federal Fair Employment Practice Committee. The committee had some success during the next eight years in addressing grievances of workers who felt that they had been discriminated against. Mary spoke to the Committee on Education and Labor on May 20, 1949, and reminded them, "An FEPC law would prohibit the taking away of one's livelihood because of his race, creed, color, national origin or ancestry. Such legislation must be quickly enacted if we are to keep faith with our fighting men and with our international statements with regard to world cooperation." However, the FEPC was considered a war measure and went out of existence in 1949.

Mary was named general of the Women's Army for National Defense and she wore her uniform with four stars for public activities. This group was like others that supported the war efforts, but this group allowed Negroes to participate, even in the segregated South. Mary was an advisor for the WACS and toured hospitals in an effort to determine how the black women were adjusting and performing in this organization. She found that the Negro women were integrated and working well with white WACS.

She met with President Roosevelt to urge him to include Negro doctors and nurses on the staffs of all institutions that cared for wounded military personnel. She reported grievances from blacks that were restricted from participating and brought to his attention incidents of violence against black servicemen in the South. She was especially upset about the Army's proposal for separate hotels for black and white veterans returning from overseas. Roosevelt listened to her reports and did what he could, ordering that there was to be no segregation in the veteran rehabilitation centers.

Mary continued to have frequent contacts with President Roosevelt and served as his advisor and friend. In 1942, she was asked by the president and Mrs. Roosevelt to bring the Bethune-Cookman quintet to entertain at a garden party for war veterans. She attended his fourth inauguration and various other civic functions as his guest.

She was delivering an address at Sam Houston State Teachers College in Dallas, Texas, when the sad news of Roosevelt's death was announced on April 12, 1945. She immediately sent Mrs. Roosevelt a wire and flew back to Washington. She was asked to speak during a radio broadcast to the nation. Here is the speech she gave to the listeners:

Others before me have spoken — others after me will speak — of the greatness of our late beloved President to this Nation of ours and the world. Let me tell you simply and sincerely what the passing of this benefactor and champion has meant to the Negro people.

He came into high office when our hearts were dragging the depths of despair. We were economically destitute — politically confused — and socially bereft of the things that make for a full American life.

He came into high office at a critical time in the lives of men and gave strength — and now his life — that all men, irrespective of their creation, should live better. It was no accident then that my people along with all other suffering minorities, should have been taken up into the arms of this humane Administrator of our government.

It was not single acts of his for which we felt so grateful as they were being unfolded. It was the largeness of his heart — the breadth of his philosophy — and the intensity of his determination.

I shall never forget that evening in the early days of his administration when he sat alone in his private office and stretched forth his gracious hand in greeting. I can hear the pathos in his voice as he said: "Hello, Mrs. Bethune, come in and sit down and tell me how your people are doing."

I poured out my heart and mind and into his ears the needs — the desires and the aspirations of my people. Since that visit, we have seen the path of our opportunities broadened into a wide thoroughfare. He believed truly that all men should have equality of opportunity regardless of race, creed, or color.

Today, we breathe a sigh — we wipe a tear — we are filled with remorse. Negroes shall confront their tomorrows with the stern resolution and conviction that he gave us in his time.

We shall not worship the past.
We shall not fear the future.
We shall carry on in the manner and in the spirit that he would have us
   do.
May God take into His household this servant.
May He protect those dearest to him who have been left behind.
And may this Nation and its people — this world — prosper in the vision
   that Franklin Delano Roosevelt saw.

She was one of two hundred family and friends who attended the funeral service in the East Room of the White House. The death of this admired personal friend affected her deeply. Later Mrs. Roosevelt gave her the President's personal monogrammed walking stick, which had been given to him by his uncle, Theodore Roosevelt. This cane became one of her prized possessions.

Chapter 6

Post-war International Involvement

"For I am my mother's daughter, and the drums of Africa still beat in my heart. They will not let me rest while there is a single Negro boy or girl without a chance to prove his worth."

Harry S. Truman took over the reins of government immediately after Roosevelt's death. He decided to move forward with the conference to draft a charter for the United Nations, which President Roosevelt had scheduled for April 25 in San Francisco. Mary was appointed as an official consultant working under Secretary of State Edward Stettinius, one of the four presiding officers. She was one of only three Negroes asked to participate as consultants. Seventy years old, her health was beginning to decline. However, she appeared at every meeting for five weeks, while conducting interviews and giving speeches at every opportunity. Mary met with other consultants in the Trustee Council, addressing such matters as the ending of martial law in occupied countries and expanding the rights of people living in colonized countries. She befriended Madame Vijaya Lakshmi Pandit from India, who later became the ambassador to the United States and a spokeswoman for the independence of her country.

Mary was disappointed with the overall accomplishments of the conference. With the two other black consultants, she composed and sent a wire to Secretary Stettinius that voiced their concerns about the lack of commitment to the freedom of those living in colonial areas as well as the failure to provide a mechanism to train citizens of newly independent countries for self-government. However, she was realistic enough to recognize that this conference was a good starting point for improvements in the

Dr. Bethune with Eleanor Roosevelt and Vijaya Lakshmi Pandit of India.

realm of international politics and government. Now, with the war over, the fight for minority rights could continue.

In 1947, Mary was seventy-two years old and her asthma problems continued to plague her; however, she remained active with her Washington activities. She did resign as president of her beloved college to let Richard V. Moore take over the reins of the college; however, she was still involved as she was named President-Emeritus, remained a member of the Board of Trustees, and served as chairwoman of the Advisory Board. The college was now a four-year college, which had earned a grade "A" in evaluation as a national institute. From a small rented house with five young girls in 1904, the school had evolved into a four-year liberal arts college with special focus on training for teachers and vocational skills. There were nineteen buildings, over 1300 students, fifty faculty members, and a campus valued at nearly two million dollars. The Harrison Rhodes Library with its 23,000 volumes was available to the public. The Moore Gymnasium with 1700 seats had been built along with tennis courts and a football field. Furthermore, white students and white faculty members were welcome, making this private institution a monument to integration in a time of segregation in the South.

In 1949, Mary was honored with an invitation from President Dumarsais Estime of Haiti to attend the Haitian Exposition. The Haitians had fought a long revolution for freedom from France, and the Americans had occupied the country to ensure peace. Franklin D. Roosevelt ended this occupation in 1934. In Haiti, Mary was given royal treatment. She toured the city of Port-au-Prince and attended a special reception in the Palace where she was awarded the Medal of Honor and Merit. This cross was the highest honor awarded by the Haitian government and Mary was the first woman to receive it.

Mary received her tenth honorary degree in 1949 when Rollins College awarded her a Doctor of Humanities degree. This was a special honor and a personal triumph for her. Twenty-two years earlier, she had been invited by the president, Hamilton Holt, to speak at the white college, but the trustees were afraid to confront the segregationist views of most of the college's supporters. To avoid problems for the young president, Mary withdrew her acceptance to speak. President Holt was retiring in 1949 and conferring this degree was to be his last official act. He took great pride in his role in making Bethune the first Negro to receive such an honor from Rollins College or, in fact, any white college in the South. She received her eleventh and final honorary degree the next year from Benedict College in Columbia, South Carolina.

Due to age and health, Mary decided to resign as the president of the National Council of Negro Women in 1949. She continued her involvement as the President Emeritus and advisor for the group. Despite her asthma and heart problems, she continued to serve on the boards of eleven more organizations. She also continued to serve as vice president of the NAACP, vice-president of the National Urban League and president of the Association for the Study of Negro Life and History. She was active in three sororities. She was a member of the Housing Board of Daytona Beach, which was committed to better the living conditions for minorities in that city. Daytona Beach awarded her the first Youth's City Award in 1951.

In 1950, Mary's home at the Bethune-Cookman College campus, her "Retreat," was made the center of a new foundation, which provided scholarships for adults and sponsored a research conference each spring and a devotional retreat each fall. An annex was added to the small house to store and preserve her files, awards, and materials.

In 1952, President Truman asked her to be one of four official delegates to Liberia to attend the second inauguration of President William Tubman. Mary was finally seeing her dream of visiting Africa come true. She nearly missed her plane when friends mistakenly took her to La Guardia Airport instead

Mary's home, the Retreat, built in 1915, later became known as the Bethune Foundation.

of the Idlewild hangar. She boarded the plane at the last minute. In Monrovia, Mary finally had a chance to see the land and people of her ancestors. She enjoyed the festivities and shook hands with 150 chiefs dressed in their tribal costumes. Bethune spent eight days in Liberia, attending the inaugural events and balls, touring the area and visiting native villages, speaking to women and starting a new branch of the National Council of Negro Women and attending formal dinners. At the final event of the visit, she received the Star of Africa award at a garden party sponsored by President Tubman.

All of this activity took its toll on her health. After an eighteen-hour flight to Paris and then a long flight back to New York, Mary spent three months in the Freedmen's Hospital recovering from severe asthma.

Dr. Frank Buchman invited her to visit Caux, Switzerland, and to attend the World Assembly for Moral Rearmament in 1954. This Assembly consisted of an international group of statesmen, students and leaders who wanted a bet-

Another view of Mary's home, the Retreat, also later known as the Bethune Foundation.

ter world. The Assembly's guiding principles were honesty, purity, unselfishness, and love, which would, hopefully, transcend country, color, and creed. Mary's main interest was racial unity, and the conference focused on ways to end segregation and focused attention on ending apartheid in South Africa. The Assembly also explored ways to change the terrorist leadership in Kenya. Confined to a wheelchair, she was pushed from place to place to meet the various delegates from around the world. She left this conference with a vision of how wonderful the world could be if all people could live in harmony and resolve differences like the international group at this conference had been able to do.

Mary returned to her home on the Bethune Cookman campus and worked on organizing her papers and her collection of mementoes gathered over her nearly eighty years of travel and experiences. Despite the fact that she usually gave her speeches without writing them down, she had a large collection of writings and letters that eventually were preserved through the efforts of the foundation that had been created for this purpose

Mary died quietly on May 18, 1955, in her home on the campus of her beloved Bethune Cookman College. After a large funeral where thousands of mourners walked by her casket to pay their respects, she was buried near her "Retreat."

Mary is at her desk in the Retreat study.

In her *Last Will and Testament*, she wrote the following:
    Sometimes as I sit communing in my study, I feel that death is not far off. I am aware that it will overtake me before the greatest of my dreams—full equality for the Negro in our times—is realized. Yet, I

face the reality without fear or regrets. I am resigned to death, as all humans must be at the proper time. Death neither alarms nor frightens one who has had a long career of fruitful toil. The knowledge that my work has been helpful to many fills me with joy and great satisfaction.

Since my retirement from an active role in educational work and from the affairs of the National Council of Negro Women, I have been living quietly and working at my desk at my home here in Florida. The years have directed a change of pace for me. I am now 76 years old and my activities are no longer so strenuous as they once were. I feel that I must conserve my strength to finish the work at hand.

Already, I have begun working on my autobiography which will record my life journey in detail, together with the innumerable side trips which have carried me abroad, into every corner of our country, into homes, both lowly and luxurious, and even into the White House to confer with the Presidents. I have also deeded my home and its contents to the Mary McLeod Bethune Foundation, organized in 1955, for research, interracial activity and sponsorship of wider educational opportunities.

Mary's grave: "She has given her best that others may live a more abundant life."

Sometimes I ask myself if I have any other legacy to leave. Truly, my worldly possessions are few. Yet my experiences have been rich. From them I have distilled principles and policies in which I believe firmly, for they present the meaning of my life's work. They are the products of much sweat and sorrow. Perhaps, in them, there is something of value. So as my life draws to a close, I will pass them on to Negroes everywhere in the hope that an old woman's philosophy may give them inspiration. Here, then, is my legacy.

I leave you love. Love builds. It is positive and helpful. Personally and racially, our enemies must be forgiven.

I leave you hope. The Negroe's growth will be great in the years to come.

I leave you the challenge of developing confidence in one another. As long as Negroes are hemmed into racial blocks of prejudice and pressure, it will be necessary for them to band together for economic betterment.

I leave you a thirst for education. Knowledge is the prime need of the hour.

I leave you faith. Faith is the first factor in life devoted to service. Without faith, nothing is possible. With it, nothing is impossible. Faith in God is the greatest power, but great too is faith in oneself.

I leave you racial dignity. I want Negroes to maintain their human dignity at all costs.

I leave you a desire to live harmoniously with your fellow man. The problem of color is worldwide. And I appeal to American Negroes, both North and South, East and West- to recognize their common problems and unite to solve them.

I leave you finally a responsibility to our young people. The world around us really belongs to youth, for youth will take over its future management. Our children must never lose their zeal for building a better world; they must not be discouraged from aspiring toward greatness, for they are to be the leaders of tomorrow.

If I have a legacy to leave my people, it is my philosophy of living and serving. As I face tomorrow, I am content, for I think I have spent my life well. I pray now that my philosophy may be helpful to those who share my vision of the world. Peace.

The statue to Mary McLeod Bethune was dedicated in 1956 in Washington, DC.

Chapter 7

Family Life

"I do feel, in my dreamings and yearnings, so undiscovered by those who are able to help me."

So much has been written about Mary Bethune's public and political life, but little has been noted about her personal life. What happened to her marriage? Her husband, Albertus, who had been a teacher, but who later entered business, tried to be supportive of her high aspirations during the first years of their marriage. But somewhere in the moves from Mayesville to Palatka to Daytona, he seems to have developed problems with achieving his own success. First, he opened a haberdashery, but that failed. He then tried tailoring, but that business also went under. His short-lived career in real estate was also a failure. In Daytona, he drove a surrey to and from the train station. Finally, when their son Albert was sent to Haines Institute, Albertus left to return to his family home in Wedgefield, South Carolina. After ten years of marriage and one son, Mary Bethune found herself alone.

However, in May 2002, grandson Albert Bethune Jr. talked of his grandfather's problems with being in Mary's shadow. Albertus was an outgoing ladies' man who had difficulty being constantly referred to as Mary's husband and forced to play a secondary role in their relationship. According to her grandson, the final straw came when Mary caught her husband with another woman and ordered him to leave their home. Public records show that Mary listed herself as a widow in the census of 1910, although Albertus did not die of tuberculosis until 1919. Divorce was such a scandalous event in those days, and she may have felt it better to be labeled a widow than to have to explain her husband's absence.

Did Mary have any other men in her life? According to one source, she attracted many suitors. On her first trip to Europe, she met several gentlemen who seemed interested in her as a woman. One persistent German begged her to marry him and an Italian also pressed her hard for her hand in marriage, referring to her as his "princess." Albert Jr. mentioned that there had been another gentleman who was "a very close friend" of his mother's. However, Mary placed her goals of the school and the need for political change above her own personal interests and nothing ever came of these relationships. Her life was devoted to helping others.

Raising her son Albert was stressful for Mary who was so involved with building her school and raising funds. In a speech given when she was seventy-nine years old and attending the World Assembly for Moral Rearmament in Caux, Switzerland, she said the following:

"I think now of my imperfections. I think of the four standards that we have as our guide here (honesty, purity, unselfishness, and love). I cannot help but express from my heart the feeling in saying how short I have been of the perfection of these standards in my humble life. I think first of my son, my only son, my only child, how I had to leave him in the care of others as I tramped all over America looking for nickels, dimes, dollars, and quarters, that I might build an institution that not only my son, but thousands of others might come. I had to neglect him. I could not give him the care, the guidance, that a tender mother needed to give a child. He often looked into my face and said, "Mother, the school come first and I come last." Now when I recognize all the defects in his life and as I have studied myself, I have analyzed these four standards we measure our lives by and I feel that my first apology is to my son Albert, who is waiting for my return."

Raising Albert was difficult for Mrs. Bethune, especially since she was increasingly busy with political activities. When he was a young man, she sent him to Miami. While working in that city, he got a white woman from Jamaica pregnant. She was ordered out of the country since it was illegal for mixed couples to have sex or marry. Albert showed up at the Mary's door carrying his seven-week old son, Albert Jr. Mary decided to adopt her own grandson as her own son. This avoided any scandalous talk about the baby's origins and also ensured that the

Dr. Bethune and her son Albert Bethune, Sr.

child's mother could not get custody of the child and take him to Jamaica. Thus, Mary now had a grandson who was her adopted son.

Mary was a strong leader, who tried to exert a positive influence in her sons' lives. This was not always the case, however, and her desire to ensure their well being sometimes went awry. Because she was gone so much of the time, she showed her love by showering the boys with expensive gifts. For example, Albert Jr. was given a brand-new Cadillac when he was in high school. This spoiled the boys and they became "womanizers like Albertus."

Mary pushed Albert Sr. to marry a very respectable young woman and he acceded to his mother's wishes. However, the marriage did not work out and he eventually became involved with another woman, who bore him five children. The older Albert was married four times. His work life was unstable as his married life and he moved from one job to another. Eventually, he became the supervisor of vocational funds at the college until a scandal caused him to resign. Albert Jr. married three times.

He and his father were not dependable in helping to run the school. Mary bought a funeral home for Albert Sr. to run, but soon he gave that up. Mary was always there to support the sons and help them out when they had problems. But there were limits to her generosity and her adopted son knew he had alienated his mother when, on the day of her death, a new will which disinherited him was discovered on her desk. She had not signed it, and thus he was still included among her heirs when her estate was settled.

Mary informally adopted another young man, Ed Rodriquez, who became like a devoted son to her. He took a strong hand in the school affairs and worked at the college until his death. Mary was close to her niece, Georgia McLeod and grandniece, Lucille Wilson, who ran the house and took care of her. Family was important to her and whenever she returned to Daytona from her many trips, the family would gather to visit her. Evelyn Bethune, the youngest grandchild, recalled how baking cookies was one way Mary used to relax. She loved to bake cookies for the young grandchildren. Evelyn remembered Mary as being very devoted to the young children in her later years. Mary would allow Evelyn to play in the kitchen cupboard while she was cooking. Evelyn could also play under Mary's desk and color pictures while Mary wrote or worked in her study. Her family referred to her as "Mother Dearest" and Mary loved that title more than all the honors she had earned. She considered the hundreds of students who had been educated at the school and whose lives she had affected as part of her extended family. In fact, most of the people who were interviewed by the author referred to her as a mother figure and many became very emotional and teary eyed as they recounted their memories of Mary and the positive influence she made in their lives.

Mary had done her best to achieve her goals. Near the end of her life, she may have felt near the end that she should have done more for her son Albert Sr. Despite this singular failure, she was an exceptional human who overcame many obstacles and achieved much by helping young people and minorities. She truly earned her esteemed role as leader and "Dearest Mother."

In the 1950's Dr. Bethune listens to the radio in her Foundation home.

Chapter 8

The Bethune Legacy:
Interviews with Mary's Children

*The man or woman who risks nothing, does nothing,
has nothing, is nothing.*

Mary McLeod Bethune was a determined and gifted educator who became famous worldwide as a political leader with high Christian principles. Today there is not a large amount of detailed information about Dr. Bethune's personal life. The former students and other individuals who have first-hand recollections of Dr. Bethune are aging and few efforts have been made to gather their stories and first-hand accounts of this great woman.

Over the past eight years, I have video-taped a number of individuals who knew Dr. Bethune and who lived in this area and were associated with the college in the 1930s, 40s and 50s. The early history of the college and even the early years of the civil rights movement in Daytona Beach were topics of discussion in the interviews.

These are some of the interviews that were conducted and recorded about Dr. Bethune and life in early Daytona. What is most impressive to this researcher is that every single interviewee presents a

In 1985, a United States postage stamp was issued in honor of Dr. Betune and her many achievements

portrait of Dr. Bethune as an amazing woman who was able to instill pride and self-confidence in those around her. Every person interviewed attributes their success and motivation in some way to Dr. Bethune's influence. All persons interviewed speak with great emotion about this woman who commanded their respect and inspired them to depart to serve as she did.

What a wonderful experience it has been to listen to those who lived through the history of the early college and knew Dr. Bethune. The goal was to capture on tape the stories of those who knew her well and to preserve these recollections for future generations. Truly, Dr. Bethune had unusual charisma and magnetism to persuade people to believe in her dreams

Listening to these individuals tell their stories has been an incredible experience for this researcher, for I relive the past through each person's recounting. These tapes are presently available at the Bethune-Cookman College Library. Dr. Bethune is gone, but her memory lives in these tales of those she so deeply affected.

These taped interviews are a trip back through time and constitute the basis for much of the factual information in this book.

FAMILY MEMBERS

Albert Bethune Sr.
The son of Mary and Albertus, he was interviewed on 10/11/82.

Leaving Palatka, Mary came to the east side of Florida in 1904 because there was nothing education-wise for Negro boys and girls in Daytona. I was five at the time and we lived with Mrs. Warren. Her three daughters were the first little girls enrolled in the school. In October 1904, the school was started in a rented building owned by John Williams, a contractor. No one thought the school would last long.

The population in Daytona was a closed society, with most of the men working in the hotels and wives as housewives. Mary brought in a music teacher, and with three other friends, they formed a quintet. Mary had one of the finest soprano voices known at that time. She took the quintet into hotels of Daytona, and that is how she met influential clientele. (Gamble from Procter & Gamble, White from White Automobiles, Endicott Johnson in the shoe business).

At the age of seven, I sang with the Girl's Chorus in a concert at the only opera house in town. I was the only boy in the Normal School for Girls, and in 5th grade I left to attend a school in Haines.

My father spent time between South Carolina and Daytona until he died in South Carolina during the flu epidemic.

Through her hotel programs, my mother met a German named Kinsey who owned the Pines Hotel and a large piece of property on 2nd Avenue. She asked to buy the land for a school, and she said she'd pay for it as she could. "That's good enough for me," said Kinsey. The only papers signed were the deed turning the land over to Mary, as Kinsey took her word and believed in her.

The land became a farm which the girls ran. They raised vegetables for canning and selling. Meat from cows, hogs, and chickens was stored for student use. Syrup cane was ground by students. Mary's brother came to the school to help the girls learn farming techniques. Mary believed in educating heart, head, and mind. Girls learned a means of livelihood.

Concerning the KKK, in 1919, there was a crucial election in which the liberal candidate Armstrong believed in the rights of all people. The KKK wanted to intimidate the Negro voters, so a large group of them marched down Second Avenue in an attempt to scare the Negroes. Meanwhile a group of Negroes and other citizens banded together and met them. KKK dispersed and the black voters, lined up for five blocks at 7:00 PM, continued to cast their votes until 1:00 AM.

Mary never panicked. As a mother she did everything she could do, considering her son and the school as the two most important things in her life. She promoted integration at a time when no other place in the South permitted it. She began Temperance meetings every Sunday at 3:00, and all members of the community would come to hear famous speakers and ideas from community members. Ushers placed people, white or black, wherever there was a vacant seat.

All of my life, I will always remember her as the one person I could go to with any problems. Drug store, hotel, funeral, my mother's influence was that she wanted me to do something for myself. But through all of that time I still kept a close connection to the college. I and three other young men formed the first quartet to travel to raise money which was so needed.

Famous people I met was Ghandi from India, Presidents Roosevelt and Truman, and President Johnson; these were some of the influential people that my mother became intrigued with.

Her most important mission including the college was Albert Bethune Sr. As busy as she might have been, there never was a time that she was too busy to know just what I was doing. I believe I was foremost in her life.

She let everybody know that she loved everybody, and she expected the same love in return.

Edward Rodrigues
Edward, or Rod as the family calls him, became like a foster son to Dr. Bethune.

A member of the family since 1923, I was the second boy to register when the school merged with the Cookman Institute. I met Mrs. Bethune in August of 1923. I was a soda jerk in her son's drugstore in Miami and had stayed out of school for several years. Mrs. Bethune said to me, "If you are willing to work, we will see you through school."

She had a great sense of humor. With her professional responsibility finished for the day, when she was relaxing at home at night, she would relate stories. One story was about Nanny Burrs, founder of the Institute for Negro Girls in Washington, who was addressing a huge audience one Sunday afternoon. With her great emotion and sweeping gestures in delivering her address, her undergarment fell to the floor, and to the great embarrassment of all, she kicked them aside and went on with her address. Of course the way Mrs. Bethune told the story, we were all in hysterics.

Mrs. Bethune served as a consultant and advisor for the Red Cross. She was in charge of choosing and referring black youths to go over seas thru the Red Cross. She was also responsible for selecting and recommending back women for the armed forces. She was then appointed the national director of NYA in 1935 for Roosevelt. Her job was to travel across the country and encourage state directors to employ black youth for the various work projects and to participate in the program of the National Youth Administration. She had a very close relationship with President Roosevelt. He told her that it was always a pleasure to have her visit, as she never asked for herself, but for others.

Albert McLeod Bethune Jr.

This adopted son/grandson of Dr. Bethune told much about the personal life of the family in this public forum at Bethune Cookman College, 2002.

My grandfather Albertus died in 1918, and I was born in 1921. There was a conflict of interest between my grandmother and grandfather. I never met him, but I will say that all the males in the Bethune family are "womanizers," my grandfather, my father, and myself. One evening Mrs. Bethune came home from a meeting with Mr. Gamble over on the beach and caught my grandfather in an compromising position with one of the workers. They broke up that day and he left that next morning and she had not seen him since. He went back to Georgia, so it was not just conflict of interest; he was caught with another woman and that is what broke up the marriage.

My own father, Albert Sr., was educated at the school along with the five little girls that Dr. Bethune began the school with. Later Albert was working in Miami when he got involved with a white woman from the islands. She gave birth to me, Albert Jr., but was then deported, as it was illegal and scandalous to have a black/white relationship at that time. My father Albert brought this 7-week-old baby boy to Dr. Bethune to raise. So now she had a grandson to care for along with the many other duties of trying to build her school. When my mother got a lawyer and tried to claim custody of me to take me to the islands to live with her, Dr. Bethune legally adopted me. Thus I, Albert Jr., became not only her grandson, but also her adopted son.

My father was in a lot of businesses. First, he had a drug store in Miami, then a hotel, and then Mrs. Bethune put us in a funeral business. The lesson is do not force your children into something they do not like. Neither my father nor I wanted to be in the funeral business. We always hired people to run it for us, such as Rabie Gainous who we hired as an embalmer. Mr. Gainous would work at the funeral home in exchange for tuition to go to the college. Later my father did get into a scandal when he was supervisor of the vocational funds at the college. He had people on the payroll who were not even registered with the college. He took $35000 of federal government money by cashing checks for people who were not with the college. Dr. Moore took over the situation and made an agreement to pay back every penny to the government. This kept my father out of jail. When my grandmother died, my father still felt that the college owed him something and should take care of him since he was Mary McLeod Bethune's son. He did get a check every month thanks to Dr. Moore.

Margaret Johnson was my stepmother. Margaret was a brilliant girl, but my father was interested in other individuals, especially a young teacher from Campbell School. However, my grandmother wanted him to marry Margaret. Acceding to her wishes, he did marry her but the marriage did not work out. I eventually took Margaret back to her father around 1952 as she had become an alcoholic.

My father and I were more like brothers as we were so close in age. We could not see the value of what Mrs. Bethune was telling us. She gave us everything. She was a loving mother who wanted the best for her sons and gave her sons anything they wanted. Mrs. Bethune absolutely loved her sons no matter what they did. She spoiled us totally. When I graduated from high school, she gave me a brand new convertible in 1939, and I tell you I was the only black kid in the whole South with such a car. She could not understand us. I was not quite as bad as my father, but I certainly had my faults too. Mrs. Bethune also took Rod who was a stock boy in my father's drug store in Miami. He was about fourteen years old. Mrs. Bethune went down to visit my dad and she brought Rod back with her. She treated him just like a foster son and made him a part of the family. Rodrigues used to sing in the quintet, and they would travel to raise funds. The Bethunes owned the whole block on Second Ave. Rod had a snack bar and there were about five stores that we owned or rented out. Mrs. Bethune could depend on Rod much more than she could depend on us.

I recall my grandmother/mother as a remarkably focused woman who would let nothing get in her way. She was not a saint, for she had a temper. She also could be very controlling, which caused my father and I myself to rebel at times. My father completed high school, but I graduated from college and library training school. Mrs. Bethune would cater to me thinking that I would do some of the things she wanted me to do, but we never did agree on that. My father and I gave our mother some real headaches with our behavior, but I always respected and admired my mother. I could be troublesome and resented her telling me what to do, but I always treated her with respect. I probably made her angry because I was pretty wild, especially because of my dealings with the young ladies. I had been accepted to Cheney College, but I went to Atlanta and met a young lady named Inez Collier who went to Spellman. So, I changed to another college to be near her, and slipped off and married her before I went off to the service in 1942. I was a womanizer just like my daddy. My daddy was married four times. I have 13 children and have been married three times. I was told that the day she died, a new copy of her will was lying on her desk to be signed, where she had been planning to cut me out of any inheritance and disown me from the estate. God blessed me for she did not sign that revised document.

There was a conflict between my father and me. I went over to the Retreat and I overheard my father speak harshly to Mrs. Bethune. He was living on the campus with this woman to whom he was not married. Mrs. Bethune wrote to a friend in Philadelphia that the embarrassment of this situation was so hard to bear, having what the community considered a scandalous situation so close to the school. I remember catching my father yelling with disrespect at her that day, and I never spoke to my father for seven years because of that.

I can laugh about it, but people must understand that my grandmother had a temper. I was in the service, and when I returned I had done something that made her so mad that she wrote me a letter saying she wished I had gotten killed in the service. When she worked with people and they did not follow what she wanted, they were not there long! She had a directness, to the point, and you did it according to Mary McLeod Bethune's plan. For example, Dr. Colson became president of the college and wanted to cut out vocational education. Mrs. Bethune was against that and Colson lasted three years. When Dr. Moore was chosen as president, she would be after him all of the time. It was hard for him to work with her, so what he did was smart. Richard Moore was a determined man who did not give up easy. He did his job the way he felt it should be done. But she remained a determined woman all of her life.

Today I attend conferences and workshops to impart my memories of her to others, especially trying to inspire youth with the ideals of my mother.

Evelyn Bethune
This daughter of Albert Sr. was a small child with memories of Mary and her last days.

My name is Evelyn Bethune and I am the granddaughter of Mary McLeod Bethune. I was born in 1952, and my father was Albert Bethune, Sr., who was Dr. Bethune's and Albertus' only son. My father was in his fifties when I was born. I attended Mainland High School. I graduated from Bethune-Cookman College in 1979 in Business and Finance, and I then worked for IBM Corporation and then had my own business for nearly 25 years. I earned a Ph.D. in political science from the University of Florida along with a master's degree in finance and political science. I lived in Boca Raton, California, and have two daughters Elizabeth and Marcia. I have a grandson Charles Jr. I have three brothers, Albert Jr. who is 82 years old, and he is the oldest living grandchild of Dr. Bethune. He has eleven children, nine boys and two girls. My sister Sara lives in Daytona Beach and she has three boys. I have two twin brothers, Hobson and Robert, who live in Jacksonville. Relatives are spread from Florida to Georgia and California. The family remains very close. We have family reunions every two years, and I talk to my siblings two to three times a week. The family stays in contact with each other.

I remember Dr. Bethune as a grandmother. I remember her as my grandmother, not an international figure. I was three years old when she passed away and I spent a great deal of time with her. She baked cookies with me and read me stories. I remember her enjoying hide and seek. My favorite hiding spot was in the cupboard under the counter that she used to bake. She lived across the street from us and when she was in town, all of us would gather at her house—grandkids, nieces and nephews, and neighbors. As soon as she would get back from her travels, we would all gather at her home.

Did she spoil me? She spoiled all of her grandkids because she did not have a lot of time to spend with us. When she was home, she would give us whatever we wanted. She did discipline us as she would not tolerate bad behavior from any of us. We knew to be on our best behavior when we went to Madear's. We followed manners and protocol. We called her "Madear," which was a shortened version of Mother Dearest.

I grew up on the college campus. That was interesting as we were always involved in educational and intellectual activities. Bethune-Cookman College was the hub of activity for black people in Daytona. All kinds of people came to campus. They would stay on campus because they were not permitted to go to beach side and stay at the hotels there. Duke Ellington, for instance, stayed at BCC because at that time he was not allowed to stay on the beach because of segregation. So as I child I was exposed to many famous people who could only stay at the campus. When she was in town, she would take this time to be with family. This was her down time and she would just enjoy the family. She did have story hours on Saturdays, and she would read stories from all over the world as all the community children would gather on the lawn to listen.

When I was three, Eleanor Roosevelt attended my birthday party. I had no idea who Eleanor Roosevelt was! At the time she was the wife of the president, but it meant nothing to me except she brought presents. My friends enjoyed it and I enjoyed it. Now as an adult I look back and think, "Wow, I had Eleanor Roosevelt at my birthday party!" That was the experience we had as being the children and grandchildren of Dr. Bethune. We just did not think much of the famous people who would come and go as it was just part of our everyday lives.

My grandmother was a very serious person much of the time because she dealt with serious issues, although she did have a great sense of humor. Most

71

of her days were spent preparing documents for a meeting here or there and preparing to travel. Running the college and being an advisor of the four presidents, she was a very busy person. But family was the center of her existence when she was home. We had to fit in as we could, but we had full access to her. She would be talking to dignitaries and politicians or being interviewed, and she would have us grandkids sitting in the room watching. She wanted us to watch and learn from the experience. As her grandkids, we were not overly impressed with title. We learned not to be so impressed with title, but it was the work a person accomplished with that title that mattered. She stressed that having the title was not as important as making the title work and doing the work.

I did not travel with Dr. Bethune alone. My parents traveled a great deal as my father was a leader in the Elks. During the 40s, 50s, and 60s he was the grand exultant ruler of the southern region. My mother was a part of the Ladies Auxiliary. My parents traveled a great deal and would often take the children.

My father was an integral part of his mother's business in terms of the school. He traveled with her when she was making trips to Washington, around the country or out of the country. He was involved with the school management so he traveled a great deal. I was always excited when he returned as he would have a gift for me with something to do with elephants as I collected them like my grandmother did. So whether it was crayon drawing or cards or an item that had an elephant on it, I always got something from my father that had to do with elephants.

Any activity with my grandmother included food, entertainment, and music. Everyone in my family sings. A lot of the funds raised for the college was through music. My father traveled and sang with the choir to raise money. My grandmother was always thinking of ways to raise funds. Many of the students were the first in their families to attend college, and they had very little money. Money was scarce and fundraising was always a concern. On these fundraising trips, my mother and my father would often take us children. We would go to Philadelphia and Chicago and a lot to Miami. My godparents were in Miami. Dr. Bethune would go to Miami a lot to meet dignitaries. We took the train to Ohio and Philadelphia. The longest train ride was when we went to California. That took some days. I was probably three or four years old.

Dr. Bethune always appeared to be well dressed and controlled in public. I do not believe my grandmother ever let her hair down with anybody, mainly because she was always on point, even with the family. There was always that feeling that she was conducting business or handling something. She always had a presence about her that was focused. She was always focused whether she was reading children stories or handling matters for the school. She always said time should never be wasted; time was something you could never get back, so never waste a moment. She always made sure that she was about the business at hand. "Stay focused" were her key words. When I heard her say that, I knew I had to stop what I was doing and get back to what I should be doing. The manner in which she conducted herself was always one of sense of purpose and direction. Many would see that as a take-charge type of person and she was. To not be in charge would be out of character for her.

She was a matriarch of our family and she was the head of our family. She was the person we looked to for advice and direction. That was understood. When she died my father took over as the person in charge of the family and then my oldest brother took over the rule. Always there was a presence of the person who was in charge of the family. She had a good sense of humor, and she had a strong sense of what God's intentions were for her.

About the college today, I feel she would be impressed with the level of education and the growth and development. The college has managed to stay financially solvent while many black colleges and universities have not. There are many wonderful programs and a beautiful campus. I think she would have a concern with the direction of the leadership. It is not as focused on a religious life as it was when she was alive. The college was founded on faith and prayer; it was founded as a school for girls to give them a sense of direction as well as to teach them to have a strong faith in God. That is not the central focus of the college today. It is still a Methodist school but I do not think she would like everything that happens there. I think she would be pleased on one hand and not pleased on the other. However, this is 2004 and things are a lot different then they were in 1904.

She took us all to church. The church was right on the corner across from our house. So anytime the light was on, we were usually there. Our family is a faith-filled family. As far as church, we are either in all the way or out—no half way. Those of us who are in have been in from the beginning, and some of us are out. Some of the family are not openly religious. We all have a strong sense of faith in God. Some of us do not believe in the strength of man as it relates to God. My grandmother prayed with us all of the time. As children we learned to pray out loud and communicate to God. She would say God listened to the smallest voice, and just pray for what you want but be willing to pay the price for what you get. God is not just for some people; he is for everyone. You do not need a translator or interpreter, but just say what is on your mind. We were taught the idea we could just talk to God and tell him what is on our mind. That is how we grew up.

Her faith in God can be described as unceasing. She drew her day-to-day strength from her faith. I do not think she could have accomplished what she did if she did not have a strong and abiding faith in God. She truly believed that if she stepped out on her faith, God would help her accomplish her goals.

That is the way she lived her live. I do not think she ever thought she could fail because she felt she was doing what God directed her to do.

I was an inquisitive child so I generally stayed in trouble because I was always investigating things and being somewhere I was not supposed to be or taking something apart. I had the run of the top floor of the library since my brother was the head librarian. I was everywhere in that library and often where I should not have been. But I never got in serious trouble as my mother watched us constantly and I had the fear that she always knew what I was doing. But inquisitive thinking, that was my niche and I carry that trait to this day. As for my grandmother, none of us ever got in trouble around her. We just enjoyed her presence when she was in town, and we were well behaved when she was around. There were a lot of kids—eleven of my brothers, four of us, and neighborhood kids, a lot of kids, but everyone knew everyone and adults watched out for the children. We were always well watched. Someone would recognize us, so we did not get into trouble much.

Dr. Bethune loved to bake cookies and her home always smelled of cookies. It was therapy for her. My favorite spot was to be in the area under her kitchen counter or to sit under her desk with a pillow and read my books. This would put me close to her because she was usually at the desk writing papers, and she would ask me, "What are you doing?" I would say reading and she would say, "Good, you keep on reading."

My grandmother would take people in. My Uncle Rodrigues was brought into the family as my grandmother would take in anyone who heeded help. He started to help with the Chorus. He taught tennis and business education. He worked with my father with vocational rehabilitation to train veterans in carpentry and vocational education, which was my father's area. Uncle Rod was a personal secretary to Dr. Bethune when she was in town. He helped to plan the travel arrangement and schedule. He died when he was 84 years old and spent most of his life on the campus. He was a part of our family even though he was not a blood relative.

I was with her near the end of her life. I believe she was most proud of Bethune-Cookman College. Next was the Council of Negro Women because it was able to pull women together from all over the world. That organization meant a great deal to her. They have continued to accomplish goals for our youth and education. Bethune-Cookman College was the crown jewel for her. She believed education was the key to success for Afro-Americans and having an institution which would help Afro Americans meet their education goals was very satisfying to her. Also to help direct the decision making and being a part of the Black Cabinet for the presidents was a great accomplishment as she had a role in shaping the road to accomplishments for Afro-Americans. Her voice helped to direct a great deal of insight and funding at the level where decisions are made and that gave her a great sense of accomplishment.

I think she was always concerned with world peace and the fact that people of color, with all of their accomplishments, were still struggling for accomplishment and an equal say. She today would not be so focused on us pursuing integration as she would focus on us pursuing economic independence.

Did she have regrets? In her last will and testament, she stated that she had no regrets. Having been the child of ex-slaves, having been a share cropper's daughter, looking back on her life, she gave a life of service not just to her people and her family, but to people all over the world.

She had an impact not just on education issues but on policy issues and how they related to people of color. I think God was well pleased with the work that she did. I would think she would be well pleased with the work she did and could see how her life affected so many people today. She is still remembered and revered in many places today. Looking back on her own life, I think that she would say "A job well done."

FORMER STUDENTS

Nellie Brown

Nellie Brown, in her late 80's, recalled how Dr. Bethune had such a profound effect on her when she was a small girl attending the school:

Dr. Bethune was the first person I had ever heard refer to the youngsters as "my beautiful black boys and girls." Dr. Bethune would say this with such love and pride that it instilled in every black child the feeling that they were special and that they could achieve great things. Dr. Bethune used to visit my parents' house often, and sit on the big swing on their porch while the mothers and children in the neighborhood would gather around for chat time. Dr. Bethune knew the people in the neighborhood well, discussed problems the people were having, and encouraged the local people to support her school and send their children there. Dr. Bethune was an integral part of the early developing city, and her contact and rapport with the locals instilled in the parents the importance of education as a way to better the lives of their children.

I do not remember segregation when I was young. We lived in a neighborhood with white people on all sides. We played together with the white children, and whenever anyone needed help in the neighborhood, such as house repairs or such, everyone helped out, regardless of color.

Idella Parker

86-years old, Idella Parker is the former maid of Marjorie Kinnans Rawling and the author of several books:

I, Idella Parker, was born and raised in Reddick, Fl, and I went to Bethune-Cookman in the late 1930's. I recall how Dr. Bethune would often sit outside on benches near the gate at 2nd Ave and talk to us girls about the importance of being a lady in speech and manner. Dr. Bethune had the straightest posture of any woman I had ever met. She always carried herself regally and was dressed formally. Dr. Bethune would always tell the girls to stand straight and tall, and she also would encourage a neat appearance and ladylike posture. Even now, I will remember those rules and I can hear Dr. Bethune's voice telling me to straighten my posture or sit properly. Dr. Bethune would often walk through and demonstrate to students the proper table manners. She would never embarrass anyone but just quietly say, "We never put our elbows on the table."

I attended Bethune for a few years but became ill, so I did not return but finished grade school at Zion near home. Then I went to Bethune for the 9th grade. The trip to Daytona took hours. There were four students who would travel in a little Chevy car and meet the Johnson girls from Kissimmee. They would travel all night, and the road was very primitive; deer and bears were a common sight. Later I returned to Bethune-Cookman for two summers, as I had to renew my certificate which allowed me to teach. In those days, if a black person had passed 8th grade and could pass the state test, the state would issue her a certificate allowing her to teach. I, with only a 9th year education, was issued a 3rd grade certificate. Four families produced many teachers who graduated from Bethune-Cookman College, and the small town, thanks to the college, produced many successful professionals, probably more educated blacks than any other little town in the area.

All the students who attended the college would work on campus to help earn their keep. Raising chickens, working in the garden, and cooking were all chores shared by students. I truly enjoyed my time at Bethune-Cookman College and my experiences there molded my life.

I later became the maid and cook for Marjorie Kinnans Rawlins. I loved living in that area, and the home and the grounds were lovely and peaceful. I have a book which Ms. Rawlins published of her southern recipes, and many of them were actually my recipes of dishes that I had prepared for her. But I went from being a maid to a writer, and now have two books published. I owe all that I have become to the lessons and inspiration that I received from Dr. Bethune and the experiences I had at Bethune-Cookman College. Dr. Bethune was like a mother to all the students. She was such an inspiration for me.

Matthew Hart

Interviewed at Ocala, FL, he was a former student and a retired educator and principal.

I met Dr. Bethune in 1930. I fell in love with her the first time I saw her at Curtis Hall as I enrolled in school. At that time, there were 75 students enrolled. Cost for tuition, room and board was $20 a month. I was hired by

Mr. Frasier in agriculture and worked on the farm. We raised chickens and had cows behind the Cookman Hall area. Anything Dr. Bethune needed, I did, whether it was gardening or security or errand boy. I remember that Dr. Bethune was "all over the place," and we never knew when she would pop into a classroom or the dorm. I would get up early in the morning to mow her lawn and do extra jobs to help pay my tuition. I had to enter the army, and then I returned to Bethune-Cookman College to finish my education. I helped build the science hall and the dining hall, and I tore down the old wooden building that had been on campus.

Water drainage was always a problem in the area. In 1932, a big storm came through and flooded the area. I remember many times after a rain, eating in the old wooden dining hall with water up to my ankles.

Monday was "work day" and everyone worked, from poor to rich students. She believed that every person needed to learn the value of work. Some classes were held on Saturday to make up for classes missed. Charles Chestnutt was one famous student I remember, and G.D. Rogers from Central Life Insurance Company was another of the wealthier students who had to cut hedges and trim trees with the rest of us. I served on the discipline committee during my six years at the college, and only one student was sent home during that time.

Dr. Bethune called me "My Dear Heart," and she was like a mother to me. I used to accompany her on her walks down Second Ave., and everyone showed such respect for her, even the "men on the juice" would straighten up and tip their hats as she walked by. Dr. Bethune had such a way of talking to people and getting them to listen to her. She could "talk a fallen tree into standing straight." I also was her chauffer when needed, and I recall driving her to the Rockefeller mansion. I remember that Rockefeller used to come to the school and give out dimes to the students and tell them to save their money and use it wisely. I got a dime from him and put it in the Bible in the center of my desk table. The next time Rockefeller came to campus, he announced that any student who still had the dimes he had given out would receive $100. I about tore that dorm building down as I raced to my room and found the dime where I had placed it, tucked in the center of my Bible. I got $100 from Rockefeller for that dime!!

Getting the money for taxes was a constant problem that Dr. Bethune faced. I would work extra hard with other students to sell produce and make extra money to help her pay taxes.

I later became a principal for 17 years. I graduated with Jimmy Huger, and when I was a principal, I would recommend students who I felt would benefit from the education and atmosphere of Bethune, and so many graduated and went on to become successful educators and business people. I kept the ideals that Dr. Bethune taught me and imparted those values in my own students, even going into the community and making students clean up their neighborhood like we had to clean up the campus. The discipline and love of students that was a part of early Bethune-Cookman College would surely improve the education of students today. The education I received from Bethune made me the success I became in life.

Reverend Golden Smith
Residing in Daytona Beach, Reverend Smith was a former student, educator and minister.

I attended Bethune-Cookman College from 1943-47. I was to attend Claflin College, but I met Dr. Bethune in Atlanta at the area council meeting of the Methodist Church. I participated in a skit for Youth Day at the council, depicting a good family and a bad family. After the skit, Dr. Bethune came to me and said, "Golden, I want you at my school." I talked to my family and made the decision to attend B-CC. At this time, Dr. Colson was president, and Dr. Bethune was very involved with the government NYA that involved getting employment for young people in America. But three times a quarter, Dr. Bethune would return to campus. I was working in her office, and I got to know her very well. I worked as her office boy, but also as a personal errand boy from her home if she needed chores done. She returned as president my senior year, and at that time I worked in her main office and she referred to me as "My Boy." I kept her office in a spic and span condition. Dr. Bethune, along with her staff, opened every workday with very emotional devotions. She saw herself as the captain and always asked God to help her lead the ship, which was Bethune- Cookman College.

I considered Dr. Bethune not only a mother to the students at BCC but also a mother to all black youth around the world. Her goal was to develop these students into world citizens who would solve any problems and contribute to the world around them. I thought about being a doctor and served part-time as an orderly at the annex, which was a facility next door to the college serving the blacks in the community. After a few months working there, I *knew* I did not want to become a doctor. Dr. Bethune told me she wanted me to become a minister. After I left Bethune-Cookman College, I went to other colleges to teach or work as dean and counselor. Dr. Bethune urged me to follow her hopes of my becoming a minister and after her death, I decided to become a preacher. Thus, I was a teacher and a minister and I continue to serve as a minister to this day.

Dr. Bethune was a great influence in my life both as an educator and a spiritual leader. She inspired me to put Christ first in my life. She made sure that I was dressed appropriately when I worked in her front office; she helped many students who had needs. She was not just a person that I knew, but also a great spiritual leader and educator; all students were inspired to emulate her. Students were not afraid of her and she would have informal visits with students at the dorm at any time. Grady James was a student who would deliver meals to her home and I would help him. I felt welcome in her home as if it were my own home. She was very stern, but caring and loving. It was a great joy to catch her by the hand and kiss her hand, and she would smile and say, "Golden, thank you." We respected her and admired her as if she were our own mother. Her secretary, Mrs. Mitchell, also cared deeply for students, and I worked during school to help in the office delivering mail and doing other chores. After school I would volunteer my time to see if there were any ways I could help as I just enjoyed her company so much during 1946-47.

She taught us to never walk over paper, but to pick it up, and she told us to greet strangers on campus in a friendly manner. She knew each student on campus by name and had a good rapport with parents.

I remember how active she was in the Methodist Church. When the Methodist Church decided to segregate the black churches into one jurisdiction, she did not pull out of the church, but she stood up and told them that this was the biggest sin the church had ever committed. After her death the church did integrate. I regret that she did not live to see that happen.

Harold Lucas

Professional football player, educator and coach, Harold Lucas was the son of the first accountant to set up the books for the college.

As a toddler, I practically grew up at the school, as my father would bring me along when he had meetings or office work. I spent a lot of time with Dr. Bethune, being friends with her grandson and having access to the house. I was well known to all the students and was the sport mascot and baseball team water boy as a youth. I replaced little Albert as the mascot, being the little kid that everyone knew. Dr. Bethune had such a charisma that a person could not help but love and admire her.

I have been in the area all my life and I have lived through all of the changes at the college. I have seen so many people come and so many changes. I recall the story I was told about when the KKK came on campus one time and Dr. Bethune was standing outside with the security guard, who was holding a shotgun. As the men marched by, one of the hooded men yelled to her, "Don't worry, Dr. Bethune, we are only marching through. We don't mean you no harm."

The building called the Manor was on the edge of the campus. Vegetables and animals were raised to help provide food for the students. White Hall was used for chapel and then when the time came for the basketball games, the chairs were set aside and the area cleared for the basketball court. There were eight buildings on campus in the 1940s. Ranslow Hall was a small practice school for the student teachers. A log cabin was a snack bar near the present cafeteria.

Cynthia Ranslow was a friend and co-worker who left money for the Ranslow Teaching Lodge built in 1947; it is still used today for offices and a classroom.

There was a scholarship given to one student who was the bell ringer. He would have to leave class a few minutes early and ring the bell in the center of the campus to tell students to change class.

BCC students had to dress in uniforms when they were off campus. This made them recognized as Dr. Bethune's children, and the community looked out for them. Dr. Bethune pushed to get blacks as policemen and bus drivers, making this one of the first areas in the South to allow this. Black bus drivers used to drive the black workers back and forth across the bridges to the beach side where many of them worked. Bethune was also involved heavily in the education system, encouraging academics but also trade skills to allow students to acquire skills they needed.

When black people of significance came to the area, they were unable to stay at the beachside hotels. Jackie Robinson and other black athletes had to stay on campus and be transported back and forth to practice, as they could not stay in the hotels on beachside. Some of the entertainers and important black people they stayed at local houses and a few small hotels in the area around the college. Sport figures were the first to be invited to go on beach side, as they were famous. News-Journal editor Davidson did a lot to help encourage integration.

When these famous people were on campus or in the area, Dr. Bethune would arrange for them to speak at the Sunday community services to the students and community to give example about what one can achieve. The message she sent out was, " If you want to be successful, you can be." Today children have so many opportunities, but in the early days of the college, there were fewer options. Dr. Bethune wanted every student to learn knowledge useful to help him or her become successful and independent. Trade was important as the college sought to train the head, heart, and the hands. The emphasis was on developing a skill that would help one succeed. Students were encouraged to follow what the teachers and counselors thought would most help them. Dr. Bethune and faculty tried to steer students to areas that best met their talents; some were helped to develop a trade that met their skills, and others might be pushed academically and encouraged to pursue higher education once they completed Bethune's two-year degree.

Dr. Bethune and the college worked for the well-rounded student. Along with development of the heart and head was the hand, meaning besides learning a useful skill, one extended the hand to help someone. She instilled in us that we did not get here by ourselves. Someone was sacrificing to get you where you are, and you should remember and give back to the community.

Juanita Jones Roberts
This Bethune graduate was interviewed in Port Orange, FL.

I was born and raised in the Daytona area. My father was a ship caulker and worked on the boats docked at the marina on the Halifax area. I remember as a youngster that the whole family would attend the Sunday community services regularly. After the services, many people would join the family for Sunday dinner, including Zora Neal Hurston, the writer who had taught at Bethune-Cookman College and who lived on a boat at that time. The people in the neighborhood attended these services without fail as they not only learned spiritual lessons, but they also were exposed to famous people and entertainers. I attended the local Campbell Elementary School and Dr. Bethune would often come as a speaker to the classes or just stop by to meet the children. I had no money for tuition to attend Bethune-Cookman College, but entered a speech contest sponsored by the Rotary Club. I won the local contest and then went on to Atlanta for the finals to learn that I was to be competing against a young man named Martin Luther King. The family I stayed with warned me that Martin would win as his father's church was one of the sponsors of the contest and he was a favorite of the judges. Martin did win, and I came in second. To this day I still feel I gave the better speech, but I concede that it is not shameful to say I finished second to Martin Luther King. The money I won in this speech contest allowed me to attend the Bethune

School, which in the early 40's was now a two-year college program.

My best memory of Dr. Bethune was when I starred as the college founder in a play about the college history. I was on stage at FAMU in Tallahassee where we performed our drama. Dr. Bethune was in the audience and came up to me afterward. "My dear," she said, "I had to keep pinching my arm to know if it was truly me in my seat or was I on stage: you were so convincing."

That was the ultimate compliment!

Clarence McClairen

This former Pittsburgh Steeler and coach came to campus when Dr. Bethune was in her late 70's.

I remember the first time I saw her was at the Sunday Community Assembly. I was sitting there sort of wishing it would be over quick. Suddenly everyone jumped to his or her feet and the activity on stage was halted. Students were craning their necks toward the middle of the aisle and all I could see was a bit of gray hair and the murmurs that Dr. Bethune was going up to the stage. "You mean the lady who founded this college?" I marveled for I had heard of her, but this was the first time she had been on campus since I arrived. I saw this short woman carrying herself with straight posture and pushing a cane rhythmically in front of herself. She began to speak to the group and I was bored no longer. She spoke with such depth and heart that even though I had already been sitting there for a long time and had only wanted to get out of the place, suddenly listening to her the time went swiftly, and I was utterly caught up in her message and emotion.

I had another encounter with Dr. Bethune later that made a deep impression. My buddies liked to horse around and play jokes on each other. One day my roommate was walking toward me and made a needling remark that he knew would cause me to respond, and I did so, using quite colorful language The roommate was setting me up, for I didn't know Dr. Bethune had come around a corner and was right behind me. Suddenly I heard a deep voice. "Young man, you are to follow me." There I was, this big strapping 6'4" football player, following behind the elderly Dr. Bethune, who would speak with me as she made her rounds to different offices. She lectured me about how young men are not supposed to talk like that and I should go to the library and study.

All morning I followed her, standing outside in the halls and going from building to building, until we finally came to the Foundation home. Then she turned to me and asked me, "Young man, will you make me a promise that you will not use that kind of language anymore?" "Yes, Ma'm," I said as I hung my head. A stick beating me on the head would not have embarrassed me or affected me any more than that experience of following her around that day and watching and listening as she traveled the campus. She was strict and disciplined, yet she disciplined or admonished others with respect, leaving them to feel the greatest admiration for her.

Dr. Bethune brought many famous people to the campus—Ralph Bunch, Jackie Robinson, Joe Louis, famous athletes, musicians, and politicians. One day the chauffer was not available to pick up Mrs. Roosevelt. I was called in since I knew how to drive and often was the driver for the football team. I remember driving across the bridge in that limousine, feeling so proud to be chauffeuring such an important woman. At the hotel, I got out to open the door for Dr. Bethune, but I was stopped by a man at the entrance who said I could not be there. Dr. Bethune got out and when the hotel man started to step forward to object, she held out her cane, gently pushed him aside, and walked past him. She went through the main entrance straight to the main desk and announced that she was there to pick up Mrs. Roosevelt. No one dared say a word to her.

When she was on campus, she would come to visit the football players at practice. There she would be surrounded by these huge football players, and she would give us a pep talk telling us that we must follow her example and never give up, no matter what the obstacles might be. She really inspired the team. She really inspired me.

James Huger

Huger was college employee for many years and a well-respected community leader, now serving as Daytona Beach city councilman.

Dr. Bethune played a major role in determining the path of my life. As a youngster, I was often on campus since my father was the financial director for the school. I later attended the college, but I ran out of money. I got a job at a hotel on beachside. My roommate would not tell anyone where I went, but then Dr. Bethune called him in; you did not lie to her. I was asleep in the hotel room when I woke up to find Dr. Bethune standing in his room asking what I was doing. I told her I needed the job to make tuition money and I had promised to work. The hotel boss was called in, and Dr. Bethune told him that she had a replacement for me; she told me I needed to get back to college and work on my degree. I pulled on my pants, packed up, followed her out of the hotel, and returned to school. I was given a job on campus and continued my studies. Dr. Bethune told me, "You are going to be somebody; I am going to see to that. So I did what she planned for me. After receiving my two-year degree from Bethune-Cookman College, I went to West Virginia State.

After graduation in 1940, I was hired to work at the War Department in Washington, D.C. I was ready to begin a new appointment when I got a call that Dr. Bethune wanted to meet with me at her office. I visited with her and she said she wanted me to work for her; she told me she had already made all the arrangements with my boss and that I was to report for work in her area the next day. I did not question her plans, and I prospered and learned working with Dr. Bethune. Later she called me in and told me all plans were made for me to return to Bethune-Cookman College, as there was need for my skills on the campus. She said, "Huger, Mrs. Mitchell, the college secretary, has too much to do. I want you to help her." I argued that I had a job already, but she said she had already taken care of everything. So I packed up and returned to Daytona.

I was working at the college when my girlfriend Fanny and I decided to get married. As a student, I had worked as a waiter under the direction of Mrs. Davis, and I had served many famous people at the private dinners at the Retreat of Dr. Bethune. After the wedding, Fanny and I had a special invitation to come for breakfast, and there we sat as the guests of honor; I was being served instead of doing the serving. It was a memorable occasion to be so honored.

When World War II broke out, I had passed the army physical but was listed as exempt since with my job at the college I was considered a professor. However, I was being kidded about being a "sissy," and I also felt guilty watching my friends go into the service. I went to Dr. Bethune and asked to be relieved of my job so that I could serve in the Marines, which had just opened to Negroes. She encouraged me to do what I felt I must, and she assured me that a job would be waiting after the war. I went to Orlando for my physical, and they told me I had "flat feet." I argued that I had passed the army physical. They consulted and decided that flat feet was a characteristic of Negroes so the Marines could accept me with that condition.

I did encounter many instances of discrimination. Even though I was a marine, in the South I would be made to ride in the "colored" train car. I became an officer, and on arrival in Washington, I was pulled over by a young military policeman who accused me of impersonating an officer because he had never seen blacks in that position before; he did not feel that I could deserve the Sergeant Major rank. He tried to arrest me, but I pulled out my credentials and my friends stood up for me and the incident passed. He ended up giving me an apology and I put him on report. But there were many occasions where prejudice was apparent in attitude and actions of the military, even though we were all fighting for democracy. My being born brown is no more my fault than you being born white. We have no control over it.

After the war, I rejoined my wife Fanny who was working as a teacher in St. Petersburg. I told Mrs. Bethune that I wanted to have my own business, so I started a filling station. It was long hours, and I found that I did not really enjoy running this business. One evening I got a phone call and Dr. Bethune said she wanted to see me the next day. I went to Daytona, and Dr. Bethune said that she had been assigned to run the United Negro College Fund, and she could not go. She wanted me to go in her place. I explained that I was "tied down" with this gas station. She told me I need not worry as she already had someone who would buy and run the gas station business; she expected me to begin work right away. Again I just followed Dr. Bethune's plans, as she always seemed to know what was best for me. I drove all the way back to St. Petersburg trying to figure out how to tell Fanny that I had to go to Washington. She was supportive. "If Dr. Bethune has enough faith in you to think that you can handle that job, then you must do it," Fanny told me.

Before the GI Bill ran out, I wanted to go to graduate school; I enrolled at the University of Michigan since Florida schools would not take blacks. Upon graduation, I was to return to my job at Bethune-Cookman College. However, I was asked to be the secretary at the National California Convention of the Alpha Phi Alpha Fraternity, and at this meeting, I was elected the national secretary for the group. I phoned Dr. Richard B Moore, who was now the president as Dr. Bethune had resigned, and told him about the election. Then I told him I would turn down the office since I was to work at the college. President Moore told me I could do more good for the college in this national position, so I accepted. This position led to many opportunities for travel and meeting people around the country, but after a while Fanny and I longed for Florida. One winter in Chicago was so cold that Fanny and I agreed that I should resign, and we returned to Daytona where I worked as an administrative assistant to Dr. Moore in 1955. Six months after I returned to Daytona, President Moore got very ill. The business manager wanted to take over, but some of the Board of Trustee members objected. President Moore left the hospital, went directly to the business manager and fired him, and named me to run the business office until he found a new manager. I remained as the business manager for twenty-eight years!

President Moore continued to expand the work that Dr. Bethune had begun. He expanded the campus, got the school accredited, and worked on building an endowment fund. Dr. Oswald Bronson followed with continuing to make the school the fine institution it is today.

I served the college until my retirement. I also was the first black to run for mayor of Daytona, and have worked as City Council member and community leader for many years. I credit Dr. Bethune with the success in my life. She was a woman of action, and she did not hesitate to do whatever was needed to acquire the people she felt would best benefit the college. She made us believe that nothing could hold us down.

Dr. Mary Alice Smith

Dr. Smith has been with Bethune-Cookman College as faculty and director of Student Support Services:

I was quite familiar with the Bethune-Cookman College before enrolling there, for I played on the campus as a child. My father, who was a minister, would attend meetings on campus, and my mother, who was a teacher, would attend classes. That was how I became acquainted with the campus, and at the same time I got to know more about Dr. Bethune. When it came time for my attending college, I was accepted at Clarke University. However, my father attended a church conference, and a minister said they needed good students to go to Bethune-Cookman College. "Where is your daughter going?" my father was asked." He replied, "Clark gave her a scholarship."

"I'll match it," said Dr. Bethune. Dr. Bethune arranged for me to take a trip to Daytona to visit the campus, and Dr. Bethune gave me a warm welcome. I fell in love with the college and was thrilled to attend Bethune-Cookman College.

I attended Bethune-Cookman College from 1944 to 1948. What I liked most about Dr. Bethune was that one could tell she was with Christ and that she had strong Christian faith. Christian music was part of the school's atmosphere. At every meal we all assembled together and sang the grade. Before breakfast, we sang:

Come with the morning hour,
Come let us kneel and pray;
Prayer is the Christian's vital breath
To walk with God all day.

Big bowls were on the table filled with grits and eggs, and students could leave when they finished. In the middle of the day was the dinner, and we would sing "Praise God From Whom All Blessings Flow." In the evening was supper, and when everyone had sat, we would sing, "If I Have Wounded Any Soul Today." In the dormitories at night, the first floor would sing the first verse of "Forgive the Sins I Have Confessed to Thee," then the second floor would sing a verse, and then the third floor would sing the last stanza. These songs were very meaningful, as you can see, since I have remembered them all these years.

Chapel meetings were another part of Christian life at Bethune-Cookman College. Dr. Bethune usually sat on the stool of a great big organ given to the school by Mr. Rockefeller. She never called a meeting just to be meeting, but meetings always had a purpose; I remember so many of the inspirational ideas and thoughts she shared with us. When Dr. Bethune walked into a room, everybody stood. Wherever we were, no matter what we were doing, when she walked in, we automatically stood.

Dr. Bethune was very sedate and gracious; she was a lady much like my mother, and I compared my mother to Dr. Bethune. Dr. Bethune's spiritual being in part came from her background. And I think she felt that when the good things came to her it was because of prayer. Dr. Bethune was a friend. She was very straightforward. She was concerned about her students and what they did and how they did after leaving Bethune-Cookman College. I especially remember one night when Dr. Bethune made a visit to the girls' dormitory. Rumor was that one of the girls had gotten pregnant, which meant immediate expulsion. Voices were hushed and all the girls watched anxiously as Dr. Bethune entered the dorm and made her way to the room of the student. Voices could be heard from behind the closed door of the girl's room, and then sobbing. After a long while, Dr. Bethune opened the door and emerged with her arm around the girl's waist and they went out of the building. Dr. Bethune handled the incident with quiet dignity and calm, and the girl was treated with understanding and compassion. The next day Dr. Bethune paid for the girl's train ticket home, and the issue was quietly ended. But always Dr. Bethune showed respect and concern for the students as individuals; students knew that they and their education were her utmost concern.

Christian service was one of the school mottoes: "Our whole school for Christian service." On Sundays, everyone gathered in the chapel for services. The chapel was used for many activities: meals, meetings, dances, basketball games, and church on Sunday. Unless a student was in the infirmary, everyone was expected to be in attendance at Sunday school and church. The community meetings were quite an experience. Attendance was mandatory and we lined up for the meeting and we were accounted for. It was a beautiful service. Persons from across the river were invited. There was usually a speaker, someone well known, but sometimes the speaking was done by the students who gave "gems" which were little sayings, insights, or memorized quotes. Dr. Bethune believed certain facts in our lives teach us to live more abundantly. One of my friends got up and recited the "purple cow" to get a laugh, and Dr. Bethune did not like it. Dr. Bethune spoke to her afterward. The choir sang many beautiful songs, such as the spirituals, anthems, and classical music. An offering was taken up at the meetings, and money was given to support the school financially.

My father was a pastor of a Methodist Church in Jacksonville. Dr. Bethune would visit once a year and talk at the church, which always brought a big crowd. Then my father died in 1949. Dr. Bethune saw me at the Jacksonville parking lot after my father had passed. Tears streamed down her face, and she told me, "I was so sorry to hear that JB had passed." She hugged me and said, "But you'll be all right," and I said, "Yes, I will be."

Dr. Bethune was an outspoken lady. She spoke the truth and was advisor to President Roosevelt and others. She had a great effect on the lives of blacks all over this country. She laid the foundation, which future presidents of the college continue to follow.

To end, I will give one of the gems that I learned at my mother's knee:

Wherever you are be noble,
Whatever you do, do well.

Whatever you speak, speak kindly
It will bring you joy and peace wherever you dwell.

Oswald Bronson
As President of Bethune-Cookman College, he gave this speech at the Bethune-Cookman College Chapel in 1999:

I came to the College in 1944. Dr. Bethune was one of history's greatest heroes. There is a simplicity to history—"her-story." Let me paraphrase the words of the poet:

Life's greatness all reminds us
We can make our lives divine
And in parting leave behind us
Footprints on the sands of time

There is, my friends, a simplicity to history. It simply means what it says. Her story—the story of Dr. Mary McLeod Bethune. Look at Dr. Bethune's footprints. She was an activist when she campaigned for voter registration, she was a patriarch asking students not to fall in the clutches of communism, a strategist to organize resources for the College, a confronter with the Klu Klux Klan on this campus, a negotiator for the United Nations under President Franklin Roosevelt and other presidents, a community worker as she labored with the Red Cross, a champion of women's rights as she worked to bring about the council of Negro women, an ambassador of divine love and justice as she witnessed for her God. Mary's footprints are evident: educator, administrator, orator activist, liberator, stateswoman, strategist, fundraiser, confrontationalist, orator, negotiator—Dr. Bethune was all of that and more.

Yet she had her weaknesses; she would be the first to say that she was not perfect. She had her frailties, her moments of regression, and her hostilities. After all, Dr. Bethune was human. The good thing about her is that she kept on marching and now she stands with Democritus, one of the greatest orators of the world, who stuttered so badly that the first time he tried to make a speech he was laughed off the rostrum.

Look at history. The great historic figures did not begin in perfection. Julius Caesar was an epileptic. Thomas Edison was deaf. Charles Dickens was lame as was Handel. Plato was a hunchback. Roosevelt's legs were paralyzed. Mary Bethune overcame abject poverty and built a school. This brings us to our view of history. Some view history as a straight line between dates and occurrences. Some view history as a hitching post. I view history as a launching pad. A hitching post ties understanding so tightly to the past that it is no good for the future.

Dr. Bethune was a launching pad. This launching pad allowed Dr. Colson to move the college from a two-year institution to a four-year college. President Moore renovated much of the campus and built Lefever Hall, the John Gross

Science Building, the library, the gymnasium and so on. Thank God Dr. Bethune's work was a launching pad, a pad that launched a multi-million dollar institution—five little girls and now alumni by the thousands. Her last will and testament spoke of the need for relevancy in the comprehensive curriculum. She was a launching pad. She spoke of the need and culture of her time. Likewise we must be relevant to the needs of our times. For example, in her day, faculty could be fired without fear of lawsuits. Sexual harassment was not in the legal vocabulary. Civil lawsuits were not part of the vocabulary. Today a lawsuit is almost assured. In her day, pregnant girls were sent home. Today we are subject to suit based on laws of discrimination. In her day, girls wore white blouses and blue skirts. Today we have to make certain some of them even wear bikinis to class. In her day when faculty members were called to her office, they would be lectured. Today they are negotiating. In her day if a student was called into the president's office, they were in trouble—now the president is in trouble.

In a more serious vein, Dr. Bethune faced very tough times. Jim Crow sat on his vicious throne condoning racial segregation: frequent lynching; courts without justice; police brutality without recourse; sharecropping without equity sharing; legislators, city commission, county council without a black representation; unfair wages; and schools unfair to children of color. In the midst of these conditions, Dr. Bethune started her school for children of color. She subscribed to the proverb that states that people do not care how much you know until they know how much you care. She could care, and her caring spirit and leadership also included patience and impatience. She was impatient with bureaucracy, with racial prejudice, with the status quo of her day, and I must admit she was impatient with those who sometimes disagreed with her. She was patient with the learners, and she knew that a good idea could grow into greatness where people were motivated and ready to move forward. She knew that a leader who has no patience with people, who is out of touch and even deluded with illusions of being in charge, would soon see his or her influence with people degrade. The evidence of strength lies not in streaking far ahead, but in adapting one's stride to meet the slower pace of the group. To go to far ahead is to lose power of influence. One writer said, "He who thinketh he leadeth and has no following is only taking a walk." Look at the multitudes still following Dr. Bethune even as she lies in her grave.

I recall I was sitting somewhere in the back of this chapel section, and Dr. Bethune would be on this platform and tell the stories about what had happened to her during the week, about people she had met at a conference with President Roosevelt, or about her ride on a train. You may have heard this story.

This was the day when they did not call a black woman "Missus," but they called her "Auntie." A conductor came up to her and said, "Auntie, are you comfortable?" She looked at him and said, "Are we related? I do not recall you being one of my sisters' or brothers' children."

There was the story of how she went into an elevator in New York, and the conductor said, "I am sorry that I cannot take you up." In those days they had the elevators that had to be cranked, and she said, "That is fine. I will take you up." And she proceeded to crank the elevator and up they went. She had a spirit or attitude against opposition. She went out to get citizens to register to vote. There are so many opportunities that we have now that they didn't have in those early days.

She would tell us how the KKK came to the Bethune campus. How she called the students to start the song "God will Take Care of You" with such beauty that the Klan rode a way. In those days, it was wrong to be too tough. But when it really comes to standing up against the crowd and declaring your faith, beliefs, and intentions, it took strength, and Mary had strength. She demanded a clean administration for us students. We as students could see a models of the values she preached. She felt it was wrong if you preach honesty, and the students see dishonesty; to preach efficiency and the students see waste; to preach harmony and the students see dissension; to teach compassion and the students experience condescension. This was a contradiction she would not tolerate. A lion and a lamb lie down together, but the lamb will not get much sleep. Why? Because the lamb does not trust the lion, and the same with the students when they see contradiction from administration verbiage.

Dr. Bethune was committed; she was an incredible person. A few years ago I had the pleasure of traveling to India where I met Mother Teresa. It was shortly after I came to this institution. It was a very moving experience. So I received from my daughter a poem that Mother Teresa had written:

People are often unreasonable, illogical, and self centered:
   Forgive them anyway.
If you are kind, people may accuse you of selfish, ulterior motives:
   Be kind anyway.
If you are successful, you will win some false friends and some true enemies:
   Succeed anyway.
If you are honest and frank, people may cheat you:
   Be honest and frank anyway.
What you spend years building, someone could destroy overnight;
   Build anyway.
If you find serenity and happiness, they may be jealous:
   Be happy anyway.
The good you do today, people will often forget tomorrow;
   Do good anyway.
Give the world the best you have, and it may never be enough;

Give the world the best you've got anyway.
You see, in the final analysis, it is between you and God:
It was never between you and them.

That is the message Mrs. Bethune also believed. So, I conclude with these words taken from the message of an African-American preacher. I will paraphrase them:

I live by faith. I walk with patience, I am uplifted by prayer, and I labor with power. My gaze is set, my gait is fast, my goal is service, my road is narrow, and my mission clear. I cannot be bought, compromised, turned back, detoured, lured away, diluted, or delayed. I will not rest in the face of sacrifice, hesitate in the face of enemies, ponder at the pool of popularity, and meander in the ways of mediocrity. I will not give up, shut up, let up — until I've stayed or stood or prayed for the cause of God. I am a disciple. I was told to become a Preacher. All I know is I will work until He stops me. When He comes, He will have no problem recognizing me for my banner is clear. I am Mary McLeod Bethune.

Juanita Gillis

Ms. Gillis is a former student and lifetime resident of Daytona Beach.

My name is Juanita Gillis and I am 75 years old. My first recollection of Dr. Bethune is following this beautiful dynamic lady and being in awe of her poise and statuesque posture. I attended Kaiser Lab. Kaiser Lab was set up at Bethune-Cookman and it was sort of an experimental school where education majors practiced and demonstrated what they had learned. I went to Kaiser Lab until 6th grade. We had to go to school on Saturday and had Mondays off. This was the most pleasant experience that I have had in my life.

Being on campus we had access to Dr. Bethune, and firsthand we saw her at breakfast, we had her come into our classroom, and on the weekends we saw her at what they called Vespers. My sister lived on campus so that gave me enormous access, and I went to Vespers on Sundays with my sister and had a chance to see Dr. Bethune beyond the classroom.

The students had to wear uniforms of navy and white and could not leave campus without this uniform. If you were a student of Bethune-Cookman College, you could be identified by your wearing the uniforms. Also, you could not leave the campus unless you were chaperoned.

We had marvelous teachers, and we got a good background on womanhood. Learning to speak well and pride in ourselves were the basic principles taught. She had one saying at the auditorium when we had chapel, and we found it amusing but it got to be her trademark, and that was that we are her "black boys and girls." She stressed morals above all else.

She was not a handsome woman by any means, but her beauty showed through her caring, her mannerisms, and her dignity. She would walk down Second Avenue with her cane because she had infirmities and was a little unsteady on her feet. And still she walked with such dignity. Her godson Rodriguez lived on the campus until his death. Her real son Albert was remarried to Elizabeth and had several children, and then he married another wife. Her son had a special liking for Angell and Phelp's chocolate, so I would be sent to get that for him. His wife was a hairdresser and they also ran a funeral home near campus. Their children lived near the campus. There were twin sons and Alva and other children whom we have kept in contact with until their deaths. It was heart warming to watch all of these grandchildren develop. People had to move because of development, and therefore I lost contact with some of them.

Students raised some of their own food on campus. The students worked with gardens and raised cows. The students had a choir that entertained for the rich whites, making appearances away from campus to spread the word of the campus life. A library was established on campus by a family named James, and that was a great contribution to the community as films and story hours and lectures were offered to the public. Having a library on campus was a great benefit because the other libraries were far away.

The WACS were stationed in Daytona and visited campus. Then housing was provided for faculty on campus. This enhanced the political life offered on campus. When Dr. Bethune was in town, we would gather round to visit her. She would talk with us and ask us if we were having any problems. I had the opportunity to serve on the campus as dorm counselor for ten years. I also worked for the community through my job in legal services. We got funding for CEDA, which helped prisoners to get rights restored and benefits for blacks. I worked to get funding for neighborhood improvements. I worked in the justice dept. to help some of the landlord and custody problems, such as not having common law established. Judge Grimes and Dr. Moore's son were some of the people with whom I was fortunate to work.

I have eight children. My father-in-law and my husband were policemen, and my son is a policeman. We were raised to be honest. Dr. Bethune influenced my life because if she could make a difference in so many lives, than I too could make a difference. This is her legacy.

She is always with me in making sure that I work to the best of my ability, never losing faith and believing that I can rise above whatever comes in my path. I was not able to finish college as my mother was ill and my father left her to raise four kids by herself.

She would explain to us that we could make a difference. Between my mother and Mrs. Bethune, I was greatly influenced and I tried to be a role model for my seven children. They all seem to care about others.

Dr. Bethune did so many wonderful things and she was such an inspiration to us. We sold fruit cakes all over the country as a fundraiser. Every year we had a production of fruit cakes in tins to keep that institution running. I had two daughters and a son-in-law in the concert chorale who traveled around the country to raise funds and promote interest in the college. I had another daughter who was able to travel to Germany and Switzerland as part of the travel experience provided by the college. Mrs. Bethune's son helped the Elks to institute an oratorical contest. I got to know Dr. Mary Alice Smith through this and we kept in contact. I have been asked to be on the Advisory Board. I continue to support the college as much as I am able. Dr. Bethune has been an inspiration to me, and I continue to serve others with her as my role model.

FACULTY AND FRIENDS

Dr. Cleo Higgins
Professor Emeritus at Bethune-Cookman College, Dr. Higgins is an expert on Dr. Bethune and she also imitates Dr. Bethune in voice and mannerism expertly.

I grew up with the Negro National Anthem; we just jumped to our feet when we heard it. I started to sing it when I was about 3 years old. It was a part of us.

I had received a degree in English from a college in Madison, Wisconsin, and then I was a teacher in Daytona. I met Dr. Bethune at a basketball game where I was coaching. I had learned so much from Dr. Bethune, and I knew her for 11 years. I knew a great deal about Ralph Waldo Emerson, who was my favorite author in literature. I loved his essay about self-reliance. I felt that Emerson's self-reliance described Dr. Bethune.

What were Dr. Bethune's spiritual underpinnings, or she might have said "undergirdings"? What was her legacy? Dr. Bethune was a great champion of justice for all people and the social issues that she served. She counseled four presidents, she traveled extensively, and she loved people.

Her spiritual underpinnings depended on faith and belief in the supreme power of God. She found a great resource in her personal dignity, her own self-esteem, and her self-confidence. She was not very tall but strongly built, and she moved with grace. She glided along: strong voice, strong tone, and strong character. I never heard her grope for words in all her speeches. She always said just the right word. She had great dignity in everything she did.

She would not let anyone disrespect her or anyone else. Part of her spiritual strength came from her concern and respect for others and her love for others. She demonstrated this in her life from the time that she realized she was the special child being the seventeenth in her large family. When her son Albert was born in 1899, he was the 90th grandchild. These three characteristics stand out: her great faith, her personal dignity, and her concern for others. I tried to transpose these in the order which most greatly influenced me. There are three things that I associate with her:

1. Giving—she gave. Giving is one of the keys to beautiful, successful, generous, rich living. There is such a joy in giving of oneself, and Dr. Bethune gave. My husband, who was a dentist practicing twenty years, went to the seminary and became a minister at Lake Butler. I used to give him ideas from items that I wrote. He would say, "That one will preach." One of these is a key to Dr. Bethune's giving. You see God so loved that he gave, giving is sharing, sharing is caring, caring is loving, and love gives. This giving is the first of the themes of Dr. Bethune's spirituality.

2. There was her constant affirmation of strength and ability that resided in her being that allowed her to rely on herself, enabling her to exude a brilliant aura of self-reliance which further served to compound her existence. For me that made her magnanimous. That self-reliance is only a firmer and deeper dependence on God. She constantly reaffirmed this.

3. She made her faith work. It wasn't just there. As I see her, it was a faith that was constantly at the test. She would say, "If it is really God's will, than I can do this; I believe that I can launch out into the deep where the big fish are. They are not near the shore."

That had a great effect on me as I started to work at Bethune-Cookman College in 1945, and I always had a group of students working on poetry and orations. I thought if I could get a little poetry into students' souls, it would go with them in their lives through bright days and bad days.

I had a very active choral speaking group in the 1970s. I was saying to the students and transmitting to them what Dr. Bethune had made me realize. I wanted them to realize that for themselves—some kind of oral transmission. I thought of myself as an agent instrumental for peace. I want to share these lines with you because these lines depict Dr. Bethune. It is a part of her basic philosophy:

To laugh is to risk appearing a fool.
To weep is to risk appearing sentimental.
To reach out to another is to risk involvement.
To expose feelings is to risk exposing your true self.
To expose your ideas, dreams, and feelings to the world is to risk loss.
To live is to risk dying.
To hope is to risk despair.
To try at all is to risk failing.
But risk we must, for the greatest hazard in life is to risk nothing.
The man or woman who risks nothing, does nothing, has nothing, is nothing.

Mrs. Bethune risked everything in life itself to pursue her dream of founding a school for girls because she was so displeased with the status of life around her. She risked family, criticism, and status, but the man, the woman who does nothing is nothing without risk.

Lastly I think that she found spiritual strength in her candor. She had a great sense of humor, twinkling hazel eyes, and in the midst of the most serious haggling within a group, she would say something so funny about herself or call something to mind that was so witty that she would calm the group down.

Howard Thurman was born in Daytona on Whitehall Street. He would come to the community services on Sundays in his knickers, and she would pat him on his head. He delivered the eulogy at the funeral in May 1955:

She had the ability to speak right to the heart of the issue while others were floundering around. She would cut right to the bone of the matter and throw people right off their feet. She did it with kindness and sternness and firmness, and she did it with laughter and humor.

She said in one speech that we are the world's problems, speaking of Negroes in religion, education and employment. The world has always wondered what to do with the Negro element. The pattern of our education was worked out for us. Someone else decided what we should study, and where we should pray. In 1949, when she was speaking to the Committee of Education and Labor, she was pleading for equal rights and equal treatment. Democratic workings were her words. Listen to the self-assertion here. She said to the chairman and committee:

"My name is Mary McLeod Bethune. I am an American and I am also a Negro. As an American I have always been imbued with the love of freedom, a belief in the rights of the individual, a respect for and loyalty to our constitutional and our constitutional form of government, and a faith in the basic principals of American fair play...It is with a great deal of concern for the well being of our country and for the protection of the spiritual and moral well being of our family, on behalf of 6.5 million Negro women, I appeal to you as our representatives of the Congress to give the right to work, dignity, and respect."

When the Supreme Court passed its decision in 1954, she said that America could now hold her head high among the nations. From within, the country had been strengthened. This was a matter of spiritual significance. We had officially declared ourselves ready to practice fully at home the doctrines of democracy, human dignity, and fairness that we have declared as a way of life.

Spirituality was engrained in everything Dr. Bethune did. It was a part of the practicality of living. To me she was a woman in action, operating on, fueled by, and sustained by the promise, "Go and I will lead you." She took him at His word. "Go and I will go with you," so she went, she risked, she gave, she affirmed, she worked.

What did she leave? What is her spiritual legacy? For me it is an awareness of what her expectations would be. These expectations were not only of students, but faculty and staff. We know this at Bethune-Cookman College. Many people still send their children to Bethune-Cookman College because they like to believe that someone in charge will have the students act as Dr. Bethune would have had them act. That kind of awareness is a part of the legacy. She wrote a piece which she called her last will and testament the year before she died. She said in this writing that she was resigned to death. She had a long career and her accomplishments filled her with great satisfaction. "I am going to will what I have and what I have experienced to those who come after me."

If you ask about religion today, she was Presbyterian. She thought the church should be active in solving problems and in helping society:

"My daily life is my temple and my religion. When you enter it, take with you your all. Take the plow, the forge, the mallet, and the lute — the things you have fashioned in necessity. Take with you all men, for you cannot fly higher than they are. Be full of hope. Humble yourself. Be not a solver of riddles. You shall see Him playing with your children. Look into space and you will see Him walking in the clouds, outstretching his arms in the lightning, descending in the rain, smiling in flowers, and then rising and waving His hands in trees."

A great source of strength she was. I found her to be the combined power of the head, the hand, and the heart. This is the motto of Bethune Cookman, which I had the great opportunity to put together in a design in 1947. She was a woman of vision, living, giving, believing and doing all based on her knowledge that her faith would make it so. "Cease to be a drudge. Think. Make yourself so busy. Take time to improve yourself so much so that you have no time to criticize others."

She had inscribed over the door of the science hall on our campus engraved in the concrete, "All science points toward God." Then she would say, "Put your hand in God's hand. But keep your feet on the ground." That makes for a pretty tall person, but that was Mrs. Bethune. She was a tall person.

Dr. Marion Speight

Dr. Marion Speight, the oldest acting faculty member at Bethune-Cookman College and possibly in the country, has fond memories of Dr. Bethune who hired Marion to work at the school in 1936.

Dr. Bethune was strict, but the students could always talk to her. She welcomed everyone in to her office. She would look you straight in the eye, and talk with you about problems you might have. She was always dignified and was treated with greatest respect by students and faculty. One day, a speaker was talking in the auditorium and going on way too long. Dr. Bethune was running late, and when the students heard the door open and she entered, they all stood up; it scared the heck out of the speaker.

She wanted the students to keep the campus clean. She would stop in class and tell the teacher to let the students out so they could clean moss off the trees. I don't know what she thought that moss was doing to those trees, eating them up, I guess, but the students would go out and do things. They ran the farm and worked in the vocational shop. She believed in preparing oneself in all areas for real life.

She was easy to get along with and had a good sense of humor. There was a bar down on Second Street. called the Black Cat. Some of the faculty were known to venture there on occasion. She would act like she could never remember the name of the person she heard was visiting there, but she'd refer to it as the Black Tiger or the Black Hole and never get the name right, but faculty would laugh and know that she did not want them to go there.

By this time in the 40s, she did not know much of what was going on in the classrooms, but she had hired a good dean to handle that for her. Likewise, she did not get involved with the finances except to solicit funds; she had hired an excellent financial manager, Mrs. Mitchell, who knew how much money was there and what to do with it.

What an eloquent speaker Dr. Bethune was, especially at the Sunday Community Services she held to bring white and blacks together for speakers and entertainment. I recall how Dr. Bethune could truly reach the audience. There w[ere] a number of stories she told about the founding of the college, and she never said the story the same way twice, but would fashion it depending on the audience. She would have poignant stories of students who needed money to attend Bethune-Cookman College. Dr. Bethune had a gift of capturing the audience emotionally and winning them over to her cause. When the collection baskets were passed, many people, tears in their eyes, would dig deep into their pockets to give support. These community services brought white and black people together at a time when nowhere else in the South was there integration. She was a great storyteller and speaker, and she appealed to the people and they would donate. Also these services introduced famous people and entertainers to the community for the common man to meet while spreading the name and goals of the college to get more support for all who attended. Dr. Bethune truly was a brilliant politician.

Most of the people who attended these Sunday meetings were white people from across the river, except for the students and some local black families. People across the river appreciated her, but many people living near the college did not seem to care much about what was happening at the college. I guess you are never appreciated in your own neighborhood. The black community thought the campus people were stuck-up. That attitude still exists today to some degree, I think. But it is improving.

She was always dressed to the hilt. Shops on beachside sent her clothes and let her try on dresses. She'd call us in to give our opinion on which dress looked better. The ones she liked, she kept, and I don't think they ever charged her for it. Of course, by this time in the 40's she was famous through her work in Washington and friendship with people like the Roosevelt's. But she surely could style a dress. I never saw her in a housedress, nightgown or a robe. She was always dressed impeccably. A niece who also kept the house prepared her meals. Albert's kids were always there keeping her company; he seemed to have another child each year, so she had lots of company.

One time a writer came to interview Bethune, and this author tried to pin the stories down and get facts. I don't think she ever did get one correct version. We faculty would watch from a balcony above while the two women interviewed each other, and the book is interesting to read, but I doubt if it tells all the right facts.

In her last years, I remember her sitting up on the balcony, watching out over the campus of her beloved school.

Dorothy Height

Dorothy is well known for her role as president emeritus of the National Council of Negro Women. At 90 years old and confined to a wheelchair, Dorothy showed remarkable energy and clarity of memory as she talked about her meeting with Dr. Bethune and working as Bethune's assistant for many years on issues and activities in Washington, DC.

My two favorite people were Dr. Bethune and Howard Thurman, and I loved to hear them speak. I worked in Washington. Then in 1937, I was given the assignment to escort Eleanor Roosevelt to a meeting with Dr. Bethune. Roosevelt drove her own [car] through the streets in Harlem and came into the back service entrance. She ignored the main entrance where others and I had prepared to meet her. I rushed to the service entrance and caught her just in time to take her into the auditorium. Later Dr. Bethune stopped me and asked me my name and she said to come back to see her as she wanted to get to know me and thought I might be helpful to her. That is how I began the rich experience of knowing Dr. Bethune.

Dr. Bethune said she needed my help. I helped Dr. Bethune work on several bills. A few years later, I went to work with her for the National Council of Negro Women. I worked during the daytime till 9:00 p.m., and then evenings and weekends I went and worked with Dr. Bethune till midnight or one o'clock. The neighborhood was safe at that time, and I would just walk the few blocks back to my apartment.

In her little apartment, Bethune would have the pound cake from Bethune-Cookman College and hot tea. She would bring in the many important men and women of the Black Cabinet for meetings. The University of North Carolina wanted an article on "what the Negro wants." Dr. Bethune called many prominent black friends to meet at her house to answer the question. After a long night of each person answering the question, she said that she knew the answer. Dr. Bethune thanked all of them for their responses and told them how great it was to have their ideas. Everyone laughed and said, "Dr. Bethune, you could have done this without us."

Later in 1942, Dr. Bethune was at a meeting of Negro women in Chicago and said that they needed a young person as executive secretary. She asked me to take that position. Before God and Dr. Bethune, I could not say no. This meant that I was able to work with her in shaping the national council. She accepted my idea that she needed to hire a professional staff to help with the work. What she envisioned and was developing required a full time staff. So I helped her to employ another executive and work was done to shape the council. From 1937 to 1957, I was a 100% volunteer in many positions and committees. For me, Dr. Bethune was a person that I could talk to personally; she was a great teacher and I learned so much from her.

Dr. Bethune was a great tea drinker, and she also enjoyed milk. During one trip to San Francisco for the founding meeting of the United Nations, Beulah Hunter Carter, who liked to sip on scotch, accompanied her. Being playful, Beulah slipped some scotch in Dr. Bethune's milk, and Dr. Bethune sipped it and kept saying it was such good milk. Beulah told her later that she had been sipping scotch, and Dr. Bethune laughed. She was asthmatic, and said that tasty milk kept her asthma under control for that trip.

After many years as the leader of the National Council of Negro Women, some of the women were voicing the opinion that Dr. Bethune was too old and that she should be replaced. When she opened the convention, she said that she heard that there were rumors that she should be replaced. "Some of you have ideas about Mary McLeod Bethune, but if you see Mary's petticoat hanging behind her, tell her, don't go telling someone else behind her back." Mary made her point and was unanimously reelected as leader of the National Council of Negro Women for another term.

Eddie Rivers

Rivers is the former Director of the Sarah Hunt Children's Home in Daytona Beach.

When people asked me how many children I had, I would say, "I have forty children." The response is always, "My lordee, did you get those all from one woman?"

Daytona Beach was like a village in those days. We were taught to give back. Everyone's mother was our mother. The Sarah Hunt Home, Mother Hunt's home, was an orphanage on Ingram Blvd., which originally was Cypress Street. A housemother was Ms. Jamison; Mildred Braxton served as a social worker. Sarah Hunt donated her house, which was a two-story building.

There were 40 or more children and a dog called Happy. When any of the children would call his name, he would smile and bare his teeth. Happy was a friend to the children for many years, and he is buried there at the home now. Daisy Stockton and Ms. Jamison helped at the home. It was an orphanage run by volunteers. There was another all white home in Enterprise. This Mother Hunt's Home was all black, and I took over the home in 1964 to 1970. Then the home came under the umbrella of the Methodist Church. I became a supervisor.

The Sarah Hunt Children's Home purchased a car to transport children. It came under the Board of Hospitals and Homes, and they wanted trained ministers and administrators. The number of children narrowed to 24 children, so some children had to go to foster homes. There were twelve children to a house. Two housemothers ran the facility. The kids called me Pop. I had to supervise, advise, and even do some spanking. When the new college was built, the two frame houses were destroyed.

Back then, I could not go into certain white congregations. We took government food and doctored it up to make it tastier. White folks would come over and want to know why our food tasted better. We blacks would take the food and we know how to season it and make it taste good.

Local stores were great support. They would send fruit and bread and other food for the children. What we couldn't use, we would give to the nursing homes in the area. The home served as a great benefit to the area. One day a girl come up to me and said, "Thank you. You helped me so much with shoes and clothes. I brought my children and you took them and kept them for three weeks and fed them. This gave me time to make my life better for me and the kids."

I traveled to Dade City, Largo, all over. I was told I couldn't go to some white churches, but I would often go and they would keep me overnight and treat me very well. The people at Enterprise took our good vehicle and gave us a beat up Volkswagen. I was forced to use that, and one trip between Jacksonville and Daytona Beach the car broke down. There I was in what then was the middle of nowhere with all of these supplies for the home weighing down the car. I went to a house and a white family let me come in and use the phone. One fellow worked and got the car running, and I was able to drive back to Daytona Beach.

Mother Hunt gave her home and land for children. She loved children. She was an amazing woman with long hair which hung nearly to the floor. After integration, the black children could go to Enterprise. The home is now used by Bethune-Cookman students. In 1968 I lost my first wife. I returned to the ministry, and I met my present sweet wife three years later.

I was born in St. Petersburg and raised in Gainesville, and I finished Clark College in 1948. After attending Atlanta Minister School, I served over 40 years as a minister.

I had heard about Dr. Bethune all of my life. I can remember the Sunday assemblies: when she walked in to the Chapel, everyone stood and sang, "Let Me Call You Sweetheart." I did not get to personally meet Dr. Bethune until the April before her death. I had the great honor of sitting next to her, and I was in my glory. She said to me, "What is your goal?" I told her that I wanted to be a minister. She just nodded and smiled at me. She had such an energy and presence; she inspired people just by her presence. I have spent my life trying to help others, and Dr. Bethune has been a great inspiration to me.

Bobbie Jean Primus-Cotton
Primus is the retired head of the Bethune-Cookman College Division of Nursing

I worked in the nursing division of Bethune, and now I work with the Committee Against HIV. My father, like Dr. Bethune, insisted on the principle of giving back to community. Our parents instilled in us the goal of going to school and never told us to stop. I remember going to the Ritz Theater on Saturdays. I never was able to see the end of the movies because I had to be home before dark. The neighborhood was family because everyone watched over the children. I can remember my second grade teacher from Cypress Street School who watched everyone coming and going. She reported every thing we did.

I remember going to the Sunday community services. We would take the bus ride, six of us, and we would ride along the river, which was such a treat. I remember that Dr. Bethune would ask for volunteers at the community service and she would "choose" her volunteers. Students had to have a gem or saying ready. They would stand and say it aloud to the group. These Sunday Services were never segregated, for all people sat where they could find a seat — regardless of their color.

Eleanor Roosevelt visited the college. My friends and I were so young and small. We were crawling under the bushes trying to sneak a look at the famous women, and suddenly Martha Mitchell who was Dr. Bethune's secretary called me to come over. I have a picture of this little pick ninny presenting Eleanor Roosevelt with a bouquet of flowers. I was that little girl!!

I can remember the black and white water fountains. My mother would not let us kids drink out of either fountain. I can remember being thirsty and wanting water, but my mother would not let us have a drink. One day I snuck a taste and found the water tasted the same from either fountain. What a disappointment?

Out of the six kids in my family, two went to Bethune Cookman. I am a FAMU graduate with a public health degree. I went on to earn my doctorate. I can still recall when I was five years old, and I attended the Kaiser Teaching Laboratory which was on campus. I remember I passed Dr. Bethune who seemed like a giant to me. She looked down on me and asked me, "Who are your people? What is your goal?" Her questions caught me by surprise. I had never thought about goals. Dr. Bethune started the first hospital for blacks west of Daytona near Tomoka for the turpentine workers. Blacks had nowhere to go before she came. Then one night one of her girls was ill with appendicitis. The city hospital at first was going to refuse the girl and finally operated on her at Dr. Bethune's insistence. After this incident, Dr. Bethune decided to open the annex on Second Ave. Blacks in the city now had a place to go. Later I visited the hospital when my sibling was born and I saw a nurse working with the newborn babies. I decided I wanted to be just like her. So the next time I saw Dr. Bethune, I told her my goal was that I was going to be a nurse. From that point I began to take care of all the sick animals and birds in the neighborhood. My career was set. Years later I remember working in the black hospital which is the present General Studies Building on campus. This was the first hospital for blacks. Later a Negro annex was established at Halifax Hospital, and I remember I ran for eight hours between the two wings which would include any patient from new babies to post operative patients. I would feel sick inside when I knew how poor our facilities were compared to what Halifax offered.

Now I am doing what the Lord wants me to do. I preach and work for the prevention of AIDS. I serve as chairperson for the Task Force on HIV/AIDS for the Women's Missionary Society of the African Methodist Episcopal Church. I have even been to Africa, and I ask that all be aware of the dangers of AIDS. One out of 50 black males are infected, and one out of 32 white males are infected. The percentage of infected females is growing rapidly. This is a ravishing disease. My promise to my father and to Dr. Bethune was that I would care for my people, and that is my call. I feel I am continuing Dr. Bethune's legacy as I work to educate people about health issues and encourage better health care for all.

"Pepper" Clifford Jenkins

One of the oldest persons interviewed was "Pepper" Clifford Jenkins, who has lived near the college since he was a toddler. Pepper is a spry 93-year old who acted and spoke like a man at least 30 years younger; he exhibited amazing wit and mental acuity for one his age. He was very modest in talking about himself, but Pepper was mentioned in other interviews by those who remember Pepper's fish and fries and his kindness when students were in need. Others talked about Pepper's unselfish help to students and his importance in the community as a leader:

My earliest memories of Dr. Bethune are when the gang of us buddies, from when we were the age of five or so, would be playing in the neighborhood. One youngster would run down the street yelling, "Mame needs some help." "Mame" is what we boys called Dr. Bethune. Soon there would be fifteen or more youngsters running at top speed over to the old building and grounds, which was the school at that time. "Mame" would tell us boys what she wanted done: clean up some branches, carry some items, any chores she needed help with. We boys eagerly would do what ever she wanted, for she instilled in us such respect. As young as I was, I was in awe of Dr. Bethune and absolutely loved her and would do anything to help her. She made each child feel special and important. She was the first person I heard call us "beautiful black boys and girls."

I never actually attended this school, which at that time was an elementary school for girls. I did support Dr. Bethune in any way I could throughout the years. I had a restaurant near the campus on 2nd Avenue (now called Dr. Mary McLeod Bethune Blvd). I knew generation after generation of students who attended the college, and my "fish and fries" were famous on campus.

I credit Dr. Bethune for serving as a role model for me, and I have tried to follow Dr. Bethune's example to serve others. Even to this day after raising my own four grandchildren, the youngest just graduating this year from high school, I try to help neighborhood children and others in the community who have problems or needs. She was a great example for me.

Mary Sheppard
Ms. Sheppard, a former business owner in Daytona Beach, was well-known for her excellent cooking.

I was raised in Georgia, and I came to Daytona Beach when I was eighteen years old. I worked across the river at different jobs. In those days blacks could only cross the river if they had a work pass. I met and married Lee Sheppard who was a landscaper. His father never wanted any of his family to work for white people and he wanted all his children to have their own business. After we got married, his father told me that I could not work on beachside for whites anymore. So in 1946, I started my own business, which was successful until the 1970s when urban renewal came. The old businesses and buildings were torn down but never rebuilt.

There were lovely businesses in New Town, which is what the area around the college was called at that time. There were ice cream parlors like the Slack Sunday Shop and restaurants such as the Gypsy Tearoom, which was the most elaborate restaurant in town for blacks since we could not go across the river. Peppers was a great chicken and fish place on Second Ave. The Jimmy Shack was a popular nightclub.

I lived next door to Mrs. Mitchell who was Dr. Bethune's secretary. My husband was a landscaper and sold dirt. He fixed lawns, and Blacks did those kinds of businesses. He didn't make that much money. Nowadays whites are doing this type of lawn care. My husband would go back in the woods and dig up bags of dirt and sell them for $1. It was such hard work for him and I don't know how we managed except for God and faith. I had my restaurant and the Bethune-Cookman College family would come to my establishment. I did most of the cooking myself. Students would pool their money and buy a few plates of chicken or dinners and split them up between themselves. I gave generous plates. President Moore would have a busload of people visiting the College and I would get a call, "Can you serve fifty people?" In an hour or so I would be serving people like Lena Horne and her band players who were visiting Bethune-Cookman College. Soul food was the specialty — chitlins, collard greens, and yams. Lena Horne loved my fried fish. There were no other place for Blacks to go, and big lines were waiting to get in on special occasions. Reverend Rogers P. Fair was a good friend and he and his friends were good customers. I never advertised and customers were my advertisers. Reverend Fair and Herbert Thompson ate there every day, and sometimes two times a day.

When I closed the restaurant, wives told me I needed to take their husbands home and feed them. I knew how the men wanted their coffee and their eggs, and they would come in every day to talk. I would feed them just what they wanted.

There were no drugs in those days, but winos were on the street. These winos actually were friends and would watch over the place. And they were always nice to me. They would come in and I would feed all of them. Many white people came to enjoy Southern food. We got by with God's help.

In 1946, a plate of beef stew cost 65 cents. That included two vegetables, rice, and yams. Chicken dinners were 75 cents. Shepard's Restaurant closed in 1971. I made $65 the first day I opened, and $450 the last day. I met people from all over: Canada to Key West. I ran into one old man recently and he said," I sure wish I had a plate of your beef stew." I looked at him and said, "So do I!" I would cook 50-60 pounds of stew a day and 50 pounds of chicken. It was hard work. When you are in business, you have five helpers and suddenly three call in sick. I would have to go down and do it myself. Some days I would be working the restaurant all by myself.

The restaurant was most prosperous in the late 40s. In the 60s with integration, the business started to fall off. Customers would try different places, but they would come back the next day because they could not get the kind of food I cooked. Those were the days! Those were good days, and I worked hard, but I felt like I was playing my role in helping people and the community. Dr. Bethune's presence as a leader and role model inspired all of us to work hard and serve others.

Pat Bennett
This former professor at a local college was the daughter on Mr. Thompson, one of the first college trustees.

My name is Patricia Thompson Bennett. I was born in Daytona Beach, which is remarkable for a person my age, and I still live on the same block, which is even more remarkable. I have many memories of Dr. Bethune. Every Christmas, the BCC choir would come and serenade us with Christmas carols. They were all dressed in white and led by Dr. Bethune. They would come by on foot, and my family and others would give them refreshments and often a donation of money.

I remember when my Aunt Lillian died, and she had donated a lot to the school. She was laid out in the dining room of Lillian Place, and Dr. Bethune came. This was 1934 and Dr. Bethune was by now well known. She entered through the back door, and she stayed in the kitchen with the servants. She was invited to come into the main dining room with the white mourners, but she simply said she would follow the social rules and stay with her fellow blacks in the kitchen area. She had such a Christian attitude. She was self-effacing and that was very unusual, very concerned for other people.

The Sunday meetings were one of the only places where whites and blacks were integrated. But segregation was a way of life. When I went to see Lena Horne in the Bethune-Cookman College chapel, all the whites sat together in front row seats, while the blacks had to sit in seats with poorer views. I was about thirteen and couldn't understand why whites were given the best seats for a black performer. I remember that Bethune Beach was the only place where blacks could go to beach. They had to be off the peninsula by dark. I could never understand this separation. My father was on the college board of trustees. He said Dr. Bethune was one of the smartest business people he had ever met. My family has always been very interested and supportive of what Dr. Bethune was doing. In fact, I'm proud to have a daughter, Mary, teaching at Bethune-Cookman College at this time.

I recall one time after Dr. Bethune had become quite well known, and she was asked to speak at Rollins College. Then because of the social attitude at the time, the invitation was withdrawn. Years later Rollins did have her come to the campus and treated her with respect. The prophet is seldom welcomed by her own.

Reverend Roger P. Fair
Reverend Fair was the chaplain for the college for over 50 years.

I was a student at Atlanta University in Georgia in 1946. Mrs. Bethune came to speak to the students, and she approached me and asked if I would like to be the minister at her college. She told me that there was an opening at a church in Daytona, and that she would speak to the bishop whom she knew well. Two weeks later I received a telegram inviting me to become the minister at this church and also asking that I become the chaplain of the college.

When I arrive in Daytona, I asked her about finances. She said that I had to be patient, and she would try to give me more than I had been receiving in

Atlanta. We became friends and I began to call her "Mom" as I felt like her son. She would inspire all of us like we had never been inspired before. I stayed in the parsonage, and then I became ill and needed a minor operation. She came to the hospital to visit, and we discussed her faith in God and how it had led her to found the college and affected its outcome. Later she personally brought food for me at the parsonage, and we talked about many things and it was a marvelous time for me.

She was so concerned about others, especially the black community who had not had opportunities. She had many ideas to organize women, and through her leadership she was able to unite thousands of people across the nation. She had great interest in good government, and this led to her advising the country's presidents. I was in her office one day when I overheard her talking on the phone to President Truman. She was recommending an individual for a position, and I will not mention his name, but he went on to become a great asset to the government.

She had a mind of her own and was not afraid of anyone, nor was she afraid to speak her mind. I loved her with all my heart. I love her now. There is a poem that I think of when I think about her.

I saw her last night
As alive as you and me.
"But you've been dead ten years?" I asked.
"I never died," said she.
"For if God lives, I live,
And I will never pass away.
I will be living in others
Who are members of the family of God.
And we will have everlasting life.
We just do not die."

Chronology

July 10, 1873:   Mary Jane McLeod is born near Mayesville, South Carolina, the fifteenth child of the former slaves Patsy and Sam McLeod.

1882:   Mary is chosen to attend a school sponsored by the Board of Missions of Freedmen. She walks five miles to and from the school daily.

1887:   After a year at home, Mary receives a scholarship to attend Scotia Seminary in Concord, North Carolina.

1894:   Mary is the only Negro to be selected to attend the Moody Bible Institute in Chicago, Illinois, where she trains to be a missionary.

1895:   Because Negroes are not permitted to be missionaries to Africa, Mary returns to the Mayesville school which she had attended; she works as an assistant teacher.

1896:   Mary moves to Atlanta, Georgia; she begins to teach at the Haines Institute.

1897:   She moves to Sumter, South Carolina, where she works at the Kindell Institute.

1898:   Mary and Albertus Bethune marry.

1899:   Only child Albert Sr. is born in February. The family moves to Palatka, Florida, to work at the Presbyterian Mission School.

October 4, 1904:   The Daytona Educational and Industrial Training School for Negro Girls opens with five students in a rented house in Daytona Beach.

1907:   The school moves to its permanent address.

1917:   Mary becomes the fourth president of the Florida Federation of Colored Women's Clubs.

1918:   White Hall is completed and dedicated on March 1.

1921:   Home for Delinquent Girls is established in Ocala by the Florida Federation of Colored Women's Clubs.

1923:   The Cookman Institute for Boys merges with the Daytona Institute forming the Bethune-Cookman Collegiate Institute.

1924:   Mary is elected president of the National Association of Colored Women.

1926:   The headquarters for the NACW is opened in Washington, D.C.

1927:   Mary tours nine countries in Europe during the summer months.

1928:   Hurricane hits Florida, and Mary organizes the rescue efforts through the American Red Cross.

1930:   She attends her first White House Conference on Child Health and Protection.

1931:   Mary is named in the top ten on Ida Tarbell's list of the fifty outstanding living American women.

1935:   The National Association of the Advancement of Colored People awards Mary the Joel E. Springarn Gold Medal for her achievements.

1935:   Mary founds the National Council of Negro Women.

1936:   She joins the Presidential Advisory Board and becomes the Director of Negro Affairs for the National Youth Administration.

1937:   The National Conference on Problems of the Negro and Negro Youth convenes: Mary delivers the "Blue Book" of recommendations to President Roosevelt.

1938:   Mary presides over the National Council of Negro Women White House Conference and the Southern Conference for Human Welfare.

1939:   The Second National Negro Conference meets.

1940:   Eleanor Roosevelt speaks at the 35th Anniversary of Bethune-Cookman College; In April, Mary has surgery for her asthma condition.

1941:   The Third National Negro Conference is held; Permanent headquarters for the Council of Negro Women is established at Vermont Ave, Washington, D.C.

1942:   At the Southern Conference for Human Welfare, Mary receives the Thomas Jefferson Award; she chooses black candidates for the Women's Army Corps. In December, she resigns as president of Bethune-Cookman College.

1943:   A general in the Women's Army for the National Defense, she is accused of being a Communist but is exonerated. She purchases Bethune Beach.

1945:   Pres. Truman names Mary a consultant to the United Nations Conference.

1946: She resumes presidency of Bethune-Cookman College but retires after one year.

1949: Mary is awarded the Medal of Honor and Merit in Haiti.

1950: The Retreat is expanded to house the Mary McLeod Bethune Foundation.

1952: She receives the Order of the Star of Africa of Liberia and tours Africa.

1954: Mary attends the World Assembly for Moral Re-Armament in Caux, Switzerland.

May 18, 1955: Mary dies of a heart attack in her Retreat home.

Index

SOURCES

Mary McLeod Bethune Papers. Mary McLeod Bethune Foundation, Bethune-Cookman College, Daytona Beach, FL.

McCluskey, Audrey & Smith, Elaine. *Mary McLeod Bethune: Building a Better World*. Bloomington: Indiana University Press, 1999.

Rackham Holt, *Mary McLeod Bethune: A Biography*. New York: Doubleday Publishing, 1964.

Peter Irons, "Jim Crow's Schools," *American Educator*. Summer 2004, p. 6.

Mary McLeod Bethune Papers. Amistad Research Center, Tulane University, New Orleans, La.

Birmingham *Reporter*. September 29, 1928.